D1467158

Game of My Life
Memorable Stories
of Packers Football

Chuck Carlson

www.SportsPublishingLLC.com

ISBN: 1-58261-814-3

© 2004 by Chuck Carlson

All rights reserved. Except for use in a review, the reproduction or utilization of this work in any form or by any electronic, mechanical, or other means, now known or hereafter invented, including xerography, photocopying, and recording, and in any information storage and retrieval system, is forbidden without the written permission of the publisher.

Publisher: Peter L. Bannon
Senior managing editor: Susan M. Moyer
Acquisitions editor: Bob Snodgrass
Developmental editor: Kipp Wilfong
Art director: K. Jeffrey Higgerson
Cover/dust jacket design: Joseph T. Brumleve
Project manager: Jim Henehan
Imaging: Kerri Baker, Christine Mohrbacher and Dustin Hubbart
Copy editor: Cynthia L. McNew
Photo editor: Erin Linden-Levy
Vice president of sales and marketing: Kevin King
Media and promotions managers: Cory Whitt (regional),
     Randy Fouts (national), Maurey Williamson (print)

Printed in the United States of America

Sports Publishing L.L.C.
804 North Neil Street
Champaign, IL 61820

Phone: 1-877-424-2665
Fax: 217-363-2073
Web site: www.SportsPublishingLLC.com

For Theresa: You're still the one.

Thanks for the advice.

Contents

Acknowledgments

M any thanks are in order for a number of people who made this book possible and, hopefully, enjoyable. First there's my old friend Bob Snodgrass, who always seems to call with another project just when I'm ready to start peeling paint off the walls in boredom. And, of course, there are the good people at Sports Publishing, and especially editor Kipp Wilfong, who have never been anything but thoroughly professional and extremely accommodating.

I'd also like to thank the public relations staff for the Green Bay Packers, featuring the ubiquitous Lee Remmel, who was recently named the team historian, as well as director of public relations Jeff Blumb and assistant director Aaron Popkey. As always, they bent over backwards to help out whenever they could.

Thanks are in order, too, to Dan Kohn, sports editor at *The Northwestern*, for diving in on short notice to copyedit and offer suggestions on a very raw, very long project. It was a big help. I'd also like to thank my wife, Theresa, and my boys, Brian, Patrick and Michael, for showing remarkable patience as I pounded away on this project and forgot they existed. I owe them a night out.

Finally, a big thank you to the Packers players who took the time out to share their stories with me. In most cases, they didn't know me from a hole in the wall, but they opened up and spoke candidly and passionately about a subject, and a time, that still matters to them. And for that I will always be appreciative.

Foreword

By Bob Harlan
President and Chief Executive Officer
The Green Bay Packers

There have been so many great games played in the history of the Green Bay Packers that I thought it might be an impossible task to single out just one. When you've been with an organization as long as I have (I started out as an assistant general manager in 1971, and it seems like just yesterday) you can recall so many great games and unforgettable moments.

As it turns out, it wasn't that difficult a decision after all.

For me it was January 12, 1997, the day the Packers beat the Carolina Panthers to win the NFC championship and earn a trip to Super Bowl XXXI in New Orleans. That was a special game in many ways for me. It was a chance to watch as this franchise, which so many people had given up on just a few years earlier, came back in such a remarkable way. It was knowing that the job so many people had done to make the Packers a contender again had been more successful than we could have dared hope.

But this was the game of my life because it was played at Lambeau Field in front of what I believe are the best fans in all of football. When I think of special games, I always come back to the fact that it should never happen in a little place like Green Bay. The thought sometimes is that special games have passed us by. But they haven't, and that game against the Panthers, played in the kind of brutally cold weather that made it even more perfect, made that point clearly.

Of course the Super Bowl victory over New England two weeks later was special as was winning the NFC championship game the following year in San Francisco. I can think of so many incredible games over the years, and they all make me smile and realize how lucky I am to be involved with a franchise like this.

But that one game on that one day summed up everything the Green Bay Packers were, are, and always will be, and I will never forget anything about it.

In *Game of My Life* you'll read about games that mattered the most, spoken in the words of the players who were there. It is a journey back in time to the games that still hold special places in the hearts and heads of Packers players who understood even then that they were part of a very special time and place. And it's a journey every Packers fan should make.

Introduction

Some memories came quickly and some memories came slowly. In some cases, they had to be coaxed out of hibernation and pried loose from places many of them hadn't visited in years. In other cases they came in torrents, almost to the point where they didn't know where to stop.

But in every case, the memories were there and ready to see daylight again. All they needed was a reason to come out again. After all, every one of them remembered the games of their lives.

"How much time do you want?" asked one ex-player when approached about the idea of reliving the greatest he ever played.

When told 20 minutes would do just fine, he laughed.

"Twenty minutes?" he said. "I don't have that kind of time."

One hour later, our interview ended.

"Thanks," he said at the conclusion. "That was fun."

Brother, was it ever.

When this journey began, the task of finding Green Bay Packers and having them recount the games of their lives seemed daunting, though not especially difficult.

After all, what player from the golden era of Vince Lombardi wouldn't automatically recount the epic "Ice Bowl" of 1967 when the Packers and Dallas Cowboys waged a war of simple survival that, at times, bore very little resemblance to a football game and was more about the best ways to avoid frostbite?

It was the game when Bart Starr snuck in for the winning touchdown that secured the Packers' second straight trip to the Super Bowl but more importantly became a part of NFL lore and legend that everyone involved in will never forget.

Or what player from the 1970s wouldn't immediately remember the Packers' 1972 NFC Central Division title, the only one the Packers won that decade?

Who from the 1980s could forget the 1983 Monday night shootout with the powerful Washington Redskins, a game that with each passing year gets a new layer of myth added to it?

And how about the 1990s when the Packers rose from the dead, won a Super Bowl and became the NFL gold standard for how to run an organization and how to treat players?

The replay game in 1989? Brett Favre's first touchdown pass in 1992? Chester Marcol's 1980 touchdown scamper against the Chicago Bears in 1979? The first Super Bowl? The second Super Bowl? Maybe the third Super Bowl?

Though this is a franchise overstuffed with great and memorable history, truly great games could be counted rather quickly, couldn't they?

The 1997 NFC title game? Lombardi's first win as Packers coach in 1959? The Monday night win over Minnesota in 2000 when Antonio Freeman caught a touchdown pass flat on his back?

How tough could it be? They think that because, for some reason, everyone figures they know the Packers better than the Packers know themselves.

Maybe it's because it's a franchise that has always made itself accessible to anyone willing to look. Maybe it's because this is a franchise that has thrived on the small-town, blue-collar ethic that makes it attractive to everyone who likes underdogs and long shots.

For whatever reason, the Packers' history has always been a book thrown open for public consumption and constant scrutiny. It also leads to the belief that everyone knows everything about this team.

But a funny thing happened. What we (OK, me) thought we knew, we did not know. What we assumed as fact was more like speculation. And what we (OK, me again) thought was the most precious of memories for Packers players wasn't close to what the conventional wisdom might have been.

It was wonderful, refreshing and surprising. And it proved one more time that we can take nothing for granted when it comes to a franchise we think we know as well as our family.

Willie Davis, the Hall of Fame defensive end, laughed when asked why he didn't mention the "Ice Bowl" as the game of his life.

"Because it really wasn't a very good game," he said simply.

When former quarterback Don Majkowski was asked why he didn't immediately jump on the "Replay Game" in 1989 as his best game, he was equally blunt.

"Because it wasn't," he said.

And isn't that the way it's supposed to be? Memories are very special and very individual and have no patent on them. What is special to one person may not even register in the brain cells of the person who was involved. And what may not have seemed particularly significant to longtime, rabid fans may never have left the minds of the players who took part.

The game of their lives is open to wonderful interpretation. There are no guidelines and no right answers. It is about the game that matters the most to the player who played the game, and that's as it should be. It isn't always about wins or losses or great performances as opposed to poor ones. It's the game that stands out above all others for its knee-buckling significance or for its ability to, in some cases, make a player still shiver in remembrance.

Great games are great games, and they will always hold their shelf lives, no matter how many years go by. Those games will take care of themselves. This book was a voyage of discovery that plumbed the depths of memories long asleep and sometimes forgotten.

Indeed, Hall of Fame guard Jerry Kramer has reveled proudly in his years with the Packers and has lost count of how many times he's talked about Vince Lombardi and the Ice Bowl. But when asked to recount the game of his life, he was taken aback.

"Nobody's ever asked me that before," he said.

Memories are a funny thing. They are personal and public; they can be full of detail or maddeningly obscure. The memories of days past can belong only to the person who lived through it, and everyone else can only watch from a distance, whether they want to or not.

In the end, *Game of My Life* is a journey back in time and, in some ways, a look forward. It is a chance to look inside the head of the player who was there and, perhaps, understand a little bit better what happened and why it happened.

To be a Green Bay Packer has always been to live under the microscope of public examination. Most of the players have understood that and dealt with it, and others have even flourished in it. But it has always been part of the game.

In the following pages, Packers from the distant past, the not-so-distant past and the present talk about the games that mattered most to them. Some will be a surprise; some will not. Hopefully they will all be entertaining.

But this much seems certain. The stories come from places most of us have never been allowed to see before, and that alone makes them special.

CHAPTER 1

JIM TAYLOR

"It was colder than any other game I played in."

Name: James Charles Taylor
Birthdate: September 20, 1935
Hometown: Baton Rouge, Louisiana
Current residence: Baton Rouge, Louisiana
Position: Fullback
Height: 6-0
Playing weight: 215
Years: 1958-66
College: LSU
Accomplishments: Was an All-America running back at LSU in 1957 and was the Packers' second-round draft pick...Rushed for more than 1,000 yards for five straight years from 1960-64...Inducted into the Pro Football Hall of Fame in 1976...Rushed for 8,207 yards, which is still the Packers' all-time leading mark...Held the record for single-season rushing record with 1,474 yards in 1962 until it was broken in 2003 by Ahman

Green…His 81 rushing touchdowns also remains a club record…NFL MVP in 1962…Named to five Pro Bowls…Was inducted into the Packers Hall of Fame in 1975.

The game: The New York Giants, December 30, 1962, at Yankee Stadium

THE LIFE OF JIM TAYLOR

The letter from the young Jim Taylor to Green Bay Packers personnel and scouting director Jim Vainisi dated November 19, 1957 was heartfelt and, perhaps, just a little desperate.

Dear Mr. Vainisi,

Reference to your letter dated November 11, 1957. I am very much interested in playing professional football. Football is a great sport and I enjoy playing it. Yes, I would be interested in playing with the Green Bay Packers. My military status is 1A Category 4. Yes, I will be able to play pro ball before entering the service. I prefer either the United States or Canada. Fullback is a position I feel I can play better.

Sincerely,
Jim Taylor
Baton Rouge, Louisiana

It was a different time and a different place and a different attitude back then. Though it was evolving quickly, football was still what you did when you were waiting to do something else with the rest of your life. Most players had off-season jobs to supplement their income because playing football did not pay all the bills. And, of course, there was always the military obligation that often forced players to leave for weeks on end to satisfy commitments to something larger than the NFL.

And Jim Taylor, the crew cut battering ram who looked like he was born with a broken nose, came out of Louisiana and was certainly no different.

Jim Taylor. *Vernon J. Biever photo*

He was already a star when he went to really the only college any self-respecting kid out of the bayou could go to—Louisiana State University, just down the road from where he grew up.

At LSU, he developed the attributes that would make him a Hall of Famer with the Packers. In today's NFL, the fullback is all but a forgotten position, manned by guys who do little more than block for the tailback and pick up blitzing linemen.

"We ran mostly between the tackles," he recalled. "You didn't run outside much then."

But back in the 1950s and '60s, all the great backs were full-backs, and they did everything from blocking to catching passes to running the ball.

Taylor joined a Packers team in 1958 that already featured Heisman Trophy winner Paul Hornung at halfback. And in those days, there were no guarantees for a second-round draft choice like Taylor.

Back then there were no high-profile and high-priced agents who negotiated staggering signing bonuses and long-term deals. More often than not, the player hammered out his own deal with the team, and it wasn't necessarily an easy process. And in the Packers' case, the player had to negotiate with a towering, intimi-dating figure like coach and general manager Vince Lombardi, who took over in 1959.

"Lombardi was tough to deal with," Taylor said. "He was very, very tough to deal with. In my first deal with him I signed for $9,500 and a $1,000 bonus, and you had to earn your position. Back then there were 34 guys on the team and I hung on and made it, but I had to do a lot of things. There's a lot more specialization now."

But by his third season, Taylor was ready to explode. He ran for 1,101 yards, scored 11 touchdowns and became the first Packer since Tony Canadeo in 1949 to rush for more than 1,000 yards. That began a streak of five straight years in which Taylor rushed for more than 1,000 yards.

But the pinnacle came in that 1962 season when Taylor ran for a league-best 1,474 yards and scored 19 touchdowns. By that stage, he was the focal point of the infamous "Packers Sweep" that was little more than a pitch to Taylor and his ability to follow the blocks of his offensive line and gain huge chunks of yardage.

"It was nothing fancy," said Taylor, who ripped off his longest run from scrimmage (83 yards) from that sweep. "We were going to make you respect it, and we defied you to stop it."

THE SETTING

It was no secret that the Packers and New York Giants hated each other in ways most people could not understand. There was jealousy, sure, that always played a role, especially since the Giants had been an established power for years while the Packers were clearly the new rising force in the NFL.

This was the Packers' third straight trip to the NFL championship game, having lost two years earlier to the Philadelphia Eagles before embarrassing the Giants 37-0 the next year in Green Bay.

"We knew they wanted revenge, but there was no jawing back and forth," Taylor said. "The AFL [the newly established American Football league] had some of that, but this was the class of the NFL and you just lined up and played the game."

The Giants went into the game with a 12-2 record, while the Packers were 13-1.

There was also plenty of gamesmanship going on, as two days before the game, coach Vince Lombardi insisted that halfback and kicker Paul Hornung was "perfect" for the game even though everyone in the Packers organization knew Hornung had no chance of playing with his knee injury.

THE GAME OF MY LIFE
By Jim Taylor

In 1961, we played the [NFL championship] in Green Bay and faced the New York Giants. We had had a pretty outstanding year and were riding high when we faced them in '61. We had beaten them that year 37-0, I think, and we went into 1962 and had another outstanding year, going 12-2 or 13-1 (it was 13-1). We were going to play the Giants again for the championship, but this time in New York.

This was the year Paul Hornung was out [with a knee injury], so we went with Tom Moore and Elijah Pitts at halfback. Jerry Kramer was doing the kicking.

I remember there were blizzard conditions at Yankee Stadium. The wind was swirling and it was 25 below zero. It was colder than any other game I ever played in. It was probably as cold as the "Ice Bowl," but you had to blank all that out and play. You poured it all out, knowing it was your last game.

It was a packed house, and they wanted revenge. They had the field covered, so it wasn't quite frozen over, but by the end of the first quarter it was. I remember we were trying on different kinds of shoes to get traction and we wondered if we should run in tennis shoes. It was tough getting anything going. I had six stitches in my elbow and I was bleeding from my mouth after being knocked out of bounds. I wasn't making a lot of yardage. It was a real hard-fought game.

They kept giving me the ball, and [Giants middle linebacker] Sam Huff kept busting my butt. There was no footing, and I kept running out of bounds. I tried to count the cheap shots Sam Huff put on me out of bounds.

In the fourth quarter, we were finally threatening to score. Bart Starr handed it off to me and I went off left tackle. Huff tackled me and said, "Taylor, you stink." Then we ran the exact same play, and I ran about seven yards. I skated into the end zone. I held up the ball and said, "Hey Sam, how do I smell from here?"

We won the game 16-7. I was brutally beat up. After that season, I came down with hepatitis and I missed the Pro Bowl. I was just run down from the end of the season, and sometimes you need rest and rejuvenation. I checked into a hospital for two weeks.

Despite a gashed elbow, Jim Taylor rushed for a rugged 85 yards and a huge touchdown in the 1962 NFL title game against the New York Giants. *Vernon J. Biever photo*

GAME RESULT

Taylor was simply spectacular in the game. Despite the gash on his elbow, which required seven stitches to close, and a lacerated tongue, compliments of Giants linebacker Sam Huff, Taylor rushed for 85 yards against the Giants in some of the worst field conditions imaginable.

The Packers led 10-0 at halftime on Taylor's touchdown run and a Jerry Kramer field goal, but the Giants got back into it in the third quarter when Jim Collier recovered a blocked punt in the end zone. But that was all the Packers defense allowed that day.

And when Kramer added his third field goal late in the fourth quarter, the Packers sewed up the game.

Neither team really did a whole lot offensively, as the Packers managed 244 total yards and the Giants 291 yards.

WHAT BECAME OF JIM TAYLOR?

After nine seasons with the Packers in which he rolled up a club-record 8,207 yards rushing, Taylor went home—back to the fledgling New Orleans Saints for the 1967 season.

It wasn't an easy decision, and it was made even more difficult by a contract battle with Vince Lombardi that Taylor knew he wasn't going to win.

It was more ceremonial than anything, as Taylor, the Louisiana kid who had made it big in the frozen north for the powerful Packers, went to a franchise just starting out.

"I was a big draw for the Saints because it was their first year," Taylor said. "It was a big deal."

Taylor's numbers weren't especially noteworthy, as he rushed for just 390 yards on 130 carries, caught 38 passes and scored two touchdowns. But that was hardly the point. Taylor was a fixture in Louisiana, and his presence made all the difference.

But he also knew that after that season, it was time to give it up. He retired and remained with the Saints as a radio color commentator and then as a traveling scout. He was named to the Pro Football Hall of Fame in 1976 and is now all but retired, though he did make a trip to Green Bay during the 2003 season when Ahman Green broke the single-season team rushing record of 1,474 yards that Taylor had established in 1962.

"I'm not envious or jealous," Taylor said of Green's accomplishment. "Any back who works that hard, you encourage them to excel. You're proud for them."

CHAPTER 2

CHESTER MARCOL

"Everything was new to me."

Name: Czeslaw Boleslaw Marcol
Birthdate: October 24, 1949
Hometown: Opole, Poland
Current residence: Dollar Bay, Michigan
Position: Kicker
Height: 6-0
Playing weight: 190
Years: 1972-80
College: Hillsdale College
Accomplishments: Inducted into the Packers Hall of Fame in 1986...NFC Rookie of the Year in 1972...All-Pro in 1972 and 1974...Pro Bowl in 1972 and 1974.
The game: Minnesota Vikings, December 10, 1972 at Metropolitan Stadium

THE LIFE OF CHESTER MARCOL

Simply, there has never been a player for the Packers like Chester Marcol. He was not the best player the Packers had ever seen, and he certainly wasn't the most athletic. But there was something about the bespectacled kicker with the thunderous right leg that made him a fan favorite then and carries on his popularity even today.

A native of Poland who spoke no English, he came to America in 1965 at the age 15 with his mother and his three siblings after his father, a member of Poland's Communist Party, committed suicide at age 39.

The family settled in little Imlay City, Michigan, where his grandparents and relatives lived, and he was forced to start a new life. After all, he left a life he loved in Poland for a country in which he didn't understand the customs or the language.

But he did understand sports and more specifically, soccer. That fall, he was asked to try out for the football team and to kick a strangely shaped ball through two upright posts. It wasn't soccer, but for a kid in a new country and a new environment, it was at least something he could make sense of.

"I said no at first," Marcol said.

But he changed his mind, and his ability to routinely kick footballs through the uprights made him a local legend. Even then, Marcol, who had been a goalkeeper on the Polish junior national team before leaving the country, didn't know what the big deal was. Kicking was second nature to him.

He took that ability down the road to Hillsdale College, where he eventually became a four-time NAIA All-American and caught the eye of the Green Bay Packers, who were desperately looking for a consist kicker. In fact, from 1968 to 1971, the Packers went through nine kickers, who among them made 45 percent of their field goals.

That's when coach Dan Devine made the stunning decision not only to draft a placekicker in the second round of the 1972

NFL Draft, but to take a placekicker no one had really heard of from a school few could find with a magnifying glass and a map. But Marcol was thrilled when the Packers selected him.

"I think it was the perfect place for me," he said. "But the Packers were the last team I thought of playing for. I could have guaranteed you that I was going to be drafted by the Dallas Cowboys. They even called me that morning and told me I was going to be drafted by them. I really wanted to play for the Cowboys because I was a sprinter and [Cowboys star wide receiver] Bob Hayes was a sprinter. The first game I ever saw was Dallas against Detroit, and I remember watching Bob Hayes."

But the Packers made the call, and it proved golden for Marcol and the Packers.

His rookie season, Marcol hit 33 of 48 field goals and led the NFL in scoring with 128 points as the Packers won their first division title since 1967. He was an All-Pro, Rookie of the Year and an NFC All-Star, and he became a favorite of Packers fans everywhere. He was every man; he was one of them. He was no product of a football factory university, and he was wonderfully lacking in ego.

THE SETTING

These were uncharted waters for the current crop of Packers. There were still some holdovers from the glory years, the fading gasp of a dynasty that grew too old too quickly. But for the most part, these were new players who knew only about the history and wanted to write their own.

Since their last burst of glory in 1967 when they won their second straight Super Bowl by plowing over the Oakland Raiders, the Packers had fallen on relatively hard times. Vince Lombardi stepped down after nine years as head coach and moved uncomfortably and unwillingly into the sole role of general manager. Taking his place in 1968 was longtime lieutenant Phil Bengston, who could not have been more different from Lombardi. Soft-spoken and professorial, Bengston struck a far different pose from the volcanic and impassioned Lombardi.

The players certainly noticed, as did Lombardi, who stayed up in the press box during games and quietly stewed. The result was a 6-7-1 season, the first losing campaign since the distasteful final days of Ray McLean in 1958 when the Packers were considered the dregs of the NFL.

Many of the same players who had been a part of the dismantling of the Raiders only months earlier in Miami—Bart Starr, Elijah Pitts, Ray Nitschke, Willie Wood, Boyd Dowler, and Dave Robinson—were still on hand this season, but it was all starting to change, and watching from high above, Lombardi could see and feel it, too.

Lombardi left the following season to become coach and general manager of the Washington Redskins and, truly, the soul of the Packers organization went with him.

Bengston had no better luck in 1969 or 1970, so the day after a demoralizing 20-0 season-ending loss to the Lions, Bengston resigned, and three weeks later Dan Devine, the head coach at the University of Missouri, was brought in.

Devine was intellectual and rather unapproachable, and players grew to either love him or despise him. But if 1971 was any indication, he was certainly no better than Bengston. Devine's fist Packers team managed a pitiful 4-8-2 record, its worst since 1958, and there seemed no reason to think anything would change in 1972. But it did.

That was Marcol's first season, and his ability to give the Packers almost automatic points from anywhere on the field took the pressure off marginal NFL quarterback Scott Hunter to have to make plays.

The offense belonged to the running back tandem of MacArthur Lane and John Brockington and a superb defense that was slowly but surely being overhauled.

The Packers got a huge dose of confidence in the season's third week when they beat the defending Super Bowl champion Dallas Cowboys 16-13 in Milwaukee and followed it up with a 20-17 win over the hated Chicago Bears thanks to Marcol's 37-yard field goal with 30 seconds to play.

The Packers closed that season strongly, routing Detroit and then clinching the division title the following week at Minnesota.

The Packers finished that season 10-4 and earned a first-round playoff game in Washington against another rejuvenated franchise. Employing an eight-man front, the Packers couldn't run anywhere, and Hunter certainly couldn't pass the Packers to victory. Though Marcol's 17-yard field goal in the second quarter gave Green Bay a 3-0 lead, the rest of the day belonged to the Redskins, as they won 16-3.

The Packers wouldn't see the postseason again until 1982 and wouldn't enjoy another division title until 1995.

THE GAME OF MY LIFE
By Chester Marcol

I don't even have to think about it. The fondest memory was in 1972 when we beat the Minnesota Vikings and won the Central Division. It was the coldest game I ever played in. I have never in my life been so cold. The field was tough, and they had a tarp on it and the heater going. The field looked like icing on a cake. That was the only time I remember wearing a ski mask under the helmet, and back then everything was so bulky that wearing that ski mask hurt my head. I remember I had difficulty taking a deep breath, it was so cold. We didn't even practice the Saturday before the game because it was so cold, and that was the only time I remember not practicing before a game.

The Vikings weren't as good as they had been, but they were still the Vikings. [Quarterback] Fran Tarkenton was still Fran Tarkenton and they had beaten us earlier in the season in Green Bay [27-13].

But I did real well. I kicked three field goals and John Brockington ran for over 100 yards. MacArthur Lane had around 90, and we beat the heck out of them, 23-7.

That was my rookie year, and that game was huge for me because every stadium I went into was a novelty. Everything was new to me. You have to remember I came from Poland and I went

Chester Marcol was the NFL Rookie of the Year in 1972 and capped a great season with three field goals in the NFC Central Division-clinching win over the Vikings. *Vernon J. Biever photo*

to Hillsdale College, so we're talking about going from something very small to something huge. It's hard to believe that was a profession. I was in awe.

There was so much excitement on the sidelines in that game. [The Met] was a stadium where you were so far away and both teams were on the same sideline line like it was at County Stadium [in Milwaukee].

I hated kicking in stadiums like that, and I give a lot of credit to the people who played before me. It was very hard to figure out the wind in stadiums like that. I remember one of the field goals I kicked in that game and I thought, "Oh no, that's five yards to the right" and when it was done it was right down the middle. On the other side of the field, it was impossible to get it there from 31 yards. And I could kick a long way.

I remember after the game we flew over [Lambeau Field] and the stadium was lit up. There were thousands of people at the airport and it took me three hours to get out of there.

We were really excited because we'd made it back to the playoffs and there was the possibility of a Super Bowl. As time goes on and with the nucleus we had, we thought we could add on to the roster and get better, but I don't know what the heck happened. We never made it back.

GAME RESULT

Since the Packers relinquished control of the NFC Central Division in 1967, the Minnesota Vikings were more than happy to fill the vacuum. Led by a solid offense and a dominating defense, the Vikings won the division from 1968 through 1971 and, after the Packers' brief interruption in 1972, took control again from 1973 to 1978.

But in 1972, it just didn't quite come together for Minnesota as it stumbled to a 7-7 record, which proved to be its worst since it was 3-8-3 in 1967.

None of that mattered to the Packers, however, who gladly took control of the division after the Vikings stumbled early out of the gate in a Monday night loss to Washington.

And this was still a dangerous and talented team, as evidenced by the fact that two months earlier the Vikings had spanked the Packers, 27-13, in Lambeau Field as Minnesota intercepted four Hunter passes. Paul Krause and Wally Hilgenberg each brought one back for a touchdown, and the Vikings' defense held the Packers' vaunted ground game to 102 yards.

Perhaps that's what made the win in Minneapolis so much sweeter. And indeed that game was far different from the one played in Green Bay.

Brockington rushed for 114 yards and Lane added 99 yards and a touchdown as the Packers took command almost from the beginning. Marcol kicked field goals of 36, 42 and 10 yards, Hunter played his typical ball-control game by completing just seven of 14 passes for 74 yards, and the defense rode two interceptions from rookie Willie Buchanon to the win. The Packers gained 270 yards in the game, and the Vikings were shut down to just 144.

WHAT BECAME
OF CHESTER MARCOL?

Marcol played nine seasons for the Packers and led the league in scoring twice. His 120 career field goals were a team record until Chris Jacke first shattered it 16 years later followed by Ryan Longwell after that.

He remained a popular figure his entire tenure in Green Bay and was the center of one of the most memorable games in Packers history.

It came on September 7, 1980, the season opener in what proved to be his final go-round with the team. Facing the Bears at Lambeau Field, Marcol had already kicked field goals of 41 and 46 yards, and the teams were tied at 6-6, forcing overtime. The Packers drove into scoring position and Marcol faced a routine 34-yard field goal that would win the game.

But Marcol's kick was blocked by Bears lineman Alan Page and the ball bounced back toward Marcol, who grabbed it out of midair and scampered, mostly out of sheer terror, into the end zone for the incredible 12-6 win.

Marcol was presented with the game ball, but few knew then the demons he was wrestling with. He had started using cocaine in training camp, and that, along with an alcohol abuse problem he had battled for years, proved a deadly combination. Overwhelmed by his addictions, his play started to suffer, and on October 8 of that season, he was released.

Out of football, he tried numerous times to clean himself up but failed. In 1986, he reached rock bottom when he drank battery acid in an attempt to kill himself. He survived and has fought his way back ever since.

He's sober now and living with his second wife, Carole, and their two kids, Mariah, 10, and Michael, seven. But life is still a struggle. He contracted hepatitis C from a blood transfusion and he has heart problems.

He helped out a local high school as a football coach for several years but now spends most of his time "collecting retirement" and fishing. He still loves Green Bay and relishes his days with the Packers.

"It's a unique environment," he said. "I have people stop by when I'm ice fishing and ask me about signing this and signing that. It was a great time."

CHAPTER 3

JESSE WHITTENTON

"I made Howard Cosell apologize."

Name: Urshell "Jesse" Whittenton
Birthdate: May 9, 1934
Hometown: Big Springs, Texas
Current residence: Santa Teresa, New Mexico
Position: Cornerback
Height: 6-0
Playing weight: 195
Years: 1958-64
College: Texas Western
Accomplishments: All-Pro 1961-62...Pro Bowl in 1961 and 1963...Inducted into Packer Hall of Fame in 1976.
The game: New York Giants, December 3, 1961 at Milwaukee County Stadium

THE LIFE OF JESSE WHITTENTON

Even before joining the Green Bay Packers in 1958 after two relatively undistinguished seasons with the Los Angeles Rams, Jesse Whittenton was no stranger to success.

A local kid from El Paso's Ysleta High School, he passed on offers from Texas and Arizona to stay close to home and play for Texas Western University, which would become Texas-El Paso. As a two-way star he helped lead the Miners to two Sun Bowl titles— whacking Southern Mississippi, 37-14 in 1954, and crushing Florida State, 47-20, in 1955.

Against Southern Miss, he caught a 29-yard touchdown pass. But against the Seminoles the following year, Whittenton had a huge game at quarterback. He threw for three touchdowns, ran for two more and kicked five extra points to account for 35 of Texas Western's 47 points. He also played defensive back.

"We were 14-point underdogs and they were pretty cocky," Whittenton said of a Florida State team that featured a halfback named Buddy Reynolds, who would one day be known as Burt Reynolds.

THE SETTING

In 1961, the Green Bay Packers were almost all the way back. It had been one of the proud, old NFL franchises that had dominated the league in the 1930s and 40s under Curly Lambeau. But after winning their sixth league championship in 1944, the Packers went through a frightful tailspin.

In the 15 years that followed, the Packers didn't get even a sniff of a championship and during a particularly black period from 1948 through 1958, the Packers never even saw the sunny side of the .500 mark. Rock bottom was reached in 1958, Whittenton's first season in Green Bay, when the Packers went 1-10-1 under Ray McLean.

"We were just awful," Whittenton said.

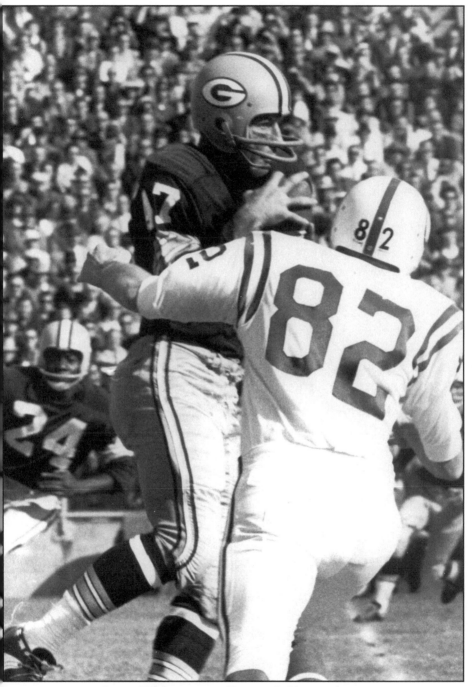

Jesse Whittenton. *Vernon J. Biever photo*

But, as has been documented so often by so many, everything started to change in 1959 when the Packers hired a former New York Giants assistant coach by the name of Vince Lombardi.

"He worked our butts off," Whittenton said. "His philosophy was always that we'll try it his way first, and if it doesn't work maybe we'll try it your way. I loved playing for him."

The results were almost immediate as the Packers went 7-5, including a season-ending four-game winning streak. In 1960, the improvement continued as Green Bay posted an 8-4 record and won its first conference title in 16 years.

In the NFL championship game December 26 at Philadelphia's Franklin Field, the Packers couldn't hold a 6-0 lead and eventually fell to the Eagles, 17-13—the only playoff loss Lombardi ever suffered.

"He told us then that we hadn't been beaten; we had just run out of time," Whittenton said. "We took that to heart."

Perhaps that's what helped the Packers in Milwaukee the next year against the Giants when they needed a huge play, somewhere, to stop New York.

That game was the first of three epic victories the Packers had over the Giants in a one-year span. Four weeks after the comeback win in Milwaukee, the Packers pounded the Giants 37-0 for their first NFL title since 1944, and the following year, the Packers beat New York again for the league title.

THE GAME OF MY LIFE
By Jesse Whittenton

The most significant game I was involved in was when we played the New York Giants in Milwaukee. We had to win that game to win the Western Conference championship.

The Giants were winning, and they were down on around our 20-yard line late in the game. [Giants running back] Alex Webster got the ball on a handoff, and he came right into the line and had enough yardage to get the first down. They could have run out the clock and won the game.

But he had the ball hanging loose in his arms, and it was just like he was handing it to me. He fumbled at around the 18-yard line, and I recovered and we went right back up the field and scored to win the game

Then in the NFL title game [on December 31] I remember I was going to be covering [Giants wide receiver] Del Shofner for most of the game. Howard Cosell said at the time that Jesse Whittenton couldn't cover [Giants star receiver] Del Shofner with a blanket. Dale caught one curl-in pass the entire game, and we beat them 37-0.

Cosell came up to me a few weeks later and said, "I'm never wrong, but I was wrong about you. You could cover Del Shofner with a blanket, and I want to apologize." I made Howard Cosell apologize.

GAME RESULT

Whittenton's remarkable play became known as the "steal," and Whittenton was nicknamed Jesse "James" Whittenton for the theft that left the Giants dazed and a little confused.

After all, the Giants were in command and needed only another first down or two to put the game away. But when Whittenton saw Webster come right at him after gaining a first down, he had only one thought.

"I went after the ball instead of the man," he said at the time, breaking one of the cardinal rules of defensive football. "It was just lucky. If I had missed it, he might have run for 10 or 15 minutes."

But he didn't miss, and the Packers took over on the Giants' 30. Five plays later, Jim Taylor stormed into the end zone from three yards out, and the Packers had the improbable victory. Afterward, Webster still didn't know what had really happened.

Taylor was magnificent again as he usually was in big games. He ran for 186 yards and two touchdowns, and Paul Hornung, who received a weekend pass from his military service in Fort Riley, Kansas, kicked two field goals and ran for another 54 yards.

Military service was mandatory those days and rarely could players get a pass like that, but when Vince Lombardi contacted President John Kennedy and told him how much the Packers needed Hornung, the pass magically appeared. However, star linebacker Ray Nitschke, who was serving at Fort Lewis, Washington, couldn't get a pass and missed the game.

WHAT BECAME OF JESSE WHITTENTON?

As much as Jesse Whittenton loved football, he loved golf that much more.

"I was a member of the Oneida Country Club [in Green Bay] and I was playing in a celebrity golf tournament back then, and I drew Vince Lombardi as my partner," Whittenton said. "I shot a 66 and he said to me, 'You're in the wrong profession.'"

He began to think that maybe Lombardi had a point, so after the 1964 season, at the still young age of 30 and with the Packers at the height of their power, he retired.

Whittenton already owned a supper club in Green Bay and made his cousin, Don Whittington, a partner. Whittenton, though a native of dusty West Texas, had grown to love Wisconsin and planned to stick around. His cousin went back to Texas and told Whittenton of an opportunity to buy a golf course near El Paso.

He asked Lombardi what he thought of the deal that called for no money down, nothing to pay monthly and free water for eight years.

"Lombardi said, 'You're not old enough to retire, but you'd be a damned fool not to take advantage of it,'" Whittenton said.

Never one to argue with his coach, he did.

Whittenton sold everything he had and bought the course in 1965 for $887,000. Whittenton and his cousin sold the course in 1969, and he's been in the golf business ever since.

In those days, he had hooked up with a young, cocky golfer named Lee Trevino, and he convinced Trevino to buy into the golf course. Those two have been friends ever since.

In the late 1980s he took a stab at joining the PGA Seniors Tour and was second alternate out of the qualifying school.

"I made just enough money to pay expenses, but I sure had a lot of fun," he said.

Despite surgeries to fix both hips, a rotator cuff and a thumb, he is still a five-handicap golfer and just recently shot his age—70.

He has rebuilt golf courses all throughout West Texas and only recently opened a driving range in El Paso that he plans to sell soon.

"I think I'll completely retire this time," he said.

CHAPTER 4

WILLIE BUCHANON

"We turned everything loose."

Name: Willie James Buchanon
Birthdate: November 4, 1950
Hometown: Oceanside, California
Current residence: Oceanside, California
Position: Cornerback
Height: 6-0
Playing weight: 190
Years: 1972-78
College: San Diego State
Accomplishments: NCAA All-American in 1971…Associated Press NFL Rookie of the Year in 1972…NFC Defensive Rookie of the Year in 1972…Inducted into Packer Hall of Fame in 1993.
The game: San Diego Chargers, September 24, 1978 at San Diego Stadium

THE LIFE OF WILLIE BUCHANON

He was one of the best athletes Oceanside, California ever produced.

A great football player and track athlete, Willie Buchanon was one of those gifted athletes that, once you saw him, you never forgot. He was an integral and popular part of the community, and anybody who knew him knew that, one day, Willie would make it big.

And they were all right.

Buchanon took his considerable football skills first to nearby MiraCosta College before going to San Diego State, where he earned All-America honors as a senior and Most Valuable Player accolades in the 1971 East-West Shrine Game.

And by then, of course, he was high on the draft board of every NFL team in the league. The Green Bay Packers were no exception. They were convinced Buchanon was a player who could make a difference immediately and dramatically. God knows they could use all the help they could get.

Green Bay was mired in a run of mediocrity it had not known since the 1950s and Devine, who was coming off a 4-8-2 record in his first season as Packers coach, knew the heat would come down hard and quickly if improvement wasn't soon.

In fact, in the four years since they had won Super Bowl II, the Packers had not retuned to the playoffs and had only one winning season. And while four substandard seasons may not have been reason for panic and angst in some NFL cities, it was not acceptable in Green Bay. Those performances had already cost Phil Bengston his job, and Devine didn't want to join him any time soon.

So the 1972 draft was huge for the Packers as they tried to put the pieces back together. And Buchanon figured to be a major part of that reconstruction project. The Packers actually had two first-round draft picks that season, and they knew they had hit it big on both of them.

Buchanon was the seventh player taken overall, the guy they hoped would be the "shutdown cornerback" before such a phrase really existed. Quick and smart and rangy, he would provide the cornerstone for a defense that was already close to being excellent but just needed another element.

The second first-rounder, and the 11th player taken overall, was Nebraska quarterback Jerry Tagge, a Green Bay native who had a superb college career but was also a product of an exceptional system. He was going to replace finally and completely the icon Bart Starr as well as the functional Scott Hunter.

To put it charitably, the Packers batted .500 on their first-round picks that year. Buchanon became everything the Packers had hoped, while Tagge...did not.

Buchanon slipped into the secondary as a rookie and played there like he'd been there forever. He finished with four interceptions and led a secondary that allowed barely 140 yards a game.

It was the season Devine, the players, and Packers fans had hoped for as they went 10-4 and won the NFC Central Division by a game and a half over the Detroit Lions. That set up the Packers' first playoff game since 1968—in Washington against the Redskins.

No one really knew it at the time, but the Packers' 16-3 loss to the Redskins would start a perplexing 10-year playoff drought that none of the players involved ever could quite figure out.

"We had the talent," Buchanon said with a sigh.

After his rookie season, Buchanon wouldn't see a winning season in Green Bay again until 1978, his final year, when they went 8-7-1 but missed out on the playoffs with two devastating losses to end the season.

Buchanon also suffered through his share of personal adversity, breaking his leg in 1973 and missing eight games and losing out on 12 more games in 1975 with another leg injury.

But those were the exceptions. On the field, he became part of a secondary that grew closer than brothers and he learned more about football and life than he ever thought he could.

Willie Buchanon. *Vernon J. Biever photo*

"I learned a lot in 1972," he said. "[Packers fullback] MacArthur Lane pulled me aside and mentored me about the NFL. He told me about coaches, agents, playing, attitude, everything. He just told me everything there was to know about the mental aspect of the game. He's still my idol and he's still probably one of the best athletes that ever played."

Ironically one of Lane's most important messages to the young cornerback was the need to look after himself.

"He told me, 'There will come a time when you're going to be just another person,'" said Buchanon, who had faith enough in his abilities to negotiate his last two pro contracts, something that's unheard of these days.

He also developed an airtight bond with his mates in the secondary—Johnnie Gray, Steve Luke and Mike McCoy.

"We called ourselves 'The Gray Zone,' because we were the guys who didn't win any [championship] rings," he said.

In his last year in Green Bay, Buchanon found he wasn't too old to learn something new. The Packers' first-round draft choice that season, an elegant wide receiver from Stanford named James Lofton, showed him just how to approach the game the way it needed to be approached.

"I never saw a wide receiver work as hard as he did," Buchanon said, marveling at it even today. "He kept me on my toes. I had to use all my knowledge to beat him."

THE SETTING

He had waited six years to play in his hometown, and when Willie Buchanon saw the Packers' schedule for 1978, he smiled. It had finally happened and he couldn't wait.

Most of Oceanside, a community 30 miles down the coast from San Diego, had followed Buchanon through his entire career. But with him playing in Wisconsin, it might as well have been Neptune, as difficult as it would have been to see him in person.

It was one of those days when everything fell into perfect alignment. The Chargers were 11-point favorites against the

Packers, even though star quarterback Dan Fouts wasn't expected to play because of a thumb injury.

But it quickly became obvious that the Packers, even in 107-degree heat, were taking this game a lot more seriously than the hosts. The Packers' offense was nothing special, and the defense knew that it might have to dominate if the Packers were going to win.

It was also a special day for Buchanon because this was a continuation of his self-styled marketing tour that would show the rest of the league that, while he was embroiled in contract woes with the Packers, he could still play the game.

And while there were no such things as free agents at that time, he was doing all he could to show all that he was one.

Buchanon also played the season for an old friend, "Chilly" Willie Walker, who had died that year.

"I dedicated that season to him," Buchanon said.

THE GAME OF MY LIFE
By Willie Buchanon

It would have to be September 24, 1978, in San Diego. That was my last year with the Green Bay Packers. I was playing out my option, and this was the first time in my career I'd returned to San Diego since I had played at San Diego State. I was hyper for the game and I was ready to play football.

I wanted to let the rest of the league know that Willlie Buchanon could still play. I was marketing myself. I wanted to stay in Green Bay, but I also wanted to let the rest of the league know I could still play. The Packers had rejected my offer, so I was playing my option without any injury protection.

I remember that date so plainly because I ended up getting four interceptions and returned one for a touchdown, and we beat the Chargers 24-3. It was 107 degrees on the football field, and the Santa Ana winds were really blowing. Fans were falling over from heat exhaustion.

I remember that the day before the game I took a picture that's still on my wall. It was of the secondary. We took it in the stadium, and it was Mike McCoy, Steve Luke and Johnnie Gray, and we said that this was my hometown and we were going to show the fans that we could play football in Green Bay. The players were playing for me and with me.

We went out there with reckless abandon and turned everything loose. I was really ready to play, and I was like that the whole season.

I grew up 35 miles down the road and I had over 300 tickets I bought for the game. All of Oceanside was there because they hadn't seen me play in that part of the country before. It was a fun event. I was looking forward to that game ever since I saw it on the schedule. We beat them really badly, and after the game [Chargers coach] Tommy Prothro was fired and Don Coryell was hired. And Don Coryell had been my college coach.

I ended up playing out the season in Green Bay and then signing with San Diego. I didn't want to leave Green Bay, and the difference was only about $25,000.

GAME RESULT

Buchanon did indeed play the game of his life at the best possible time. Those four interceptions, one of which was taken back 77 yards for the touchdown that accounted for the final margin, remains a Packers record until this day. Perhaps even more important, though, is that two of those interceptions came in the end zone to squelch Chargers drives.

For whatever reason, the Chargers had no clue that day against the Packers. Starting quarterback James Harris threw two interceptions, forcing Prothro to insert the ailing Fouts, who fired two more interceptions of his own. Even the No. 3 quarterback, some guy by the name of Cliff Olander, got into the charity by throwing the fifth interception of the game. That last one went to Buchanon, who took it back 77 yards for the score with 2:16 to play.

Buchanon of course was the star, with the four interceptions that tied an NFL record and which remains a Packers record he shares with Bobby Dillon. But Buchanon also added nine unassisted tackles in the game.

The Chargers completely disintegrated in the game, not only flinging five interceptions but losing six fumbles and managing just 245 total yards.

"It was a disaster," Prothro wailed afterward.

Packers coach Bart Starr wasn't all that thrilled with his team's offensive performance, either. Quarterback David Whitehurst completed just seven of 14 passes for 92 yards. Amazingly, the Packers won easily, despite gaining only 127 yards on offense.

WHAT BECAME
OF WILLIE BUCHANON?

The great Willie Buchanon marketing tour of 1978 worked superbly. He finished with nine interceptions that season and, when contract talks continued to go nowhere, the Packers traded him to the Chargers following the season for a first- and seventh-round draft pick. He was reunited with his old college coach, Don Coryell.

Buchanon found himself hip-deep in one of the NFL's most prolific and entertaining teams—especially on offense. It was a team that featured quarterback Dan Fouts, tight end Kellen Winslow and a jailbreak offense called affectionately (and otherwise) "Air Coryell."

But for all the pyrotechnics of that offense and for all the games those Chargers won, they never made it to the Super Bowl. Buchanon played four seasons for the Chargers before retiring.

He stayed in the San Diego area and became a successful real estate broker. With his partner, Mark Stone, Buchanon recently started another real estate company, Stonemark Properties.

But there is so much more to the postfootball Willie Buchanon. He went back and has taught history and geography in every school—from elementary to college—he ever attended. He also helps coach track at his high school alma mater, Oceanside High School; he is the music minister at his church, and he is involved in numerous charities around the country.

He also takes a father's pride in his son, William, who is a wide receiver at the University of Southern California and whom Willie has tutored more than a little.

And he still thinks often about Green Bay and the team he never really wanted to leave in the first place.

"I would have taken $150,000 from the Packers, and they told me they couldn't pay me that because I'd be the second highest player on the team behind Lynn Dickey," he said with bemusement. "I wanted to stay there with my defense, but I have no regrets."

And to this day, he has nothing but good feelings about his Green Bay years.

"It was truly the best football-playing town in America," he said. "The fans and the stadium—it was all about playing football. Green Bay really gave you an opportunity to concentrate on playing football."

Then he laughed again.

"There was nothing else to do."

CHAPTER 5

JERRY KRAMER

"It was a hell of a football game."

Name: Gerald Louis Kramer
Birthdate: January 23, 1936
Hometown: Jordan, Montana
Current residence: Parma, Idaho
Position: Offensive guard
Height: 6-3
Playing weight: 245
Years: 1958-68
College: University of Idaho
Accomplishments: All-Pro in 1960-63 and 1967-68...Named to Pro Bowl in 1962, 1963 and 1967...Named to Packers All-Time Modern Era team, All-Century team and 50th Anniversary Team...Inducted into Packer Hall of Fame in 1975...Author of five books, including the bestselling *Instant Replay* in 1968.
The game: New York Giants, December 30, 1962 at Yankee Stadium

THE LIFE OF JERRY KRAMER

Jerry Kramer was always something a little more than a football. Urbane and witty, he came from the mountains of Idaho with a view of the world and of life that made him one of the great spokesmen for the Lombardi-era Packers.

He was, of course, the superb right guard known more for the block that sprung Bart Starr on that epic quarterback sneak in the "Ice Bowl." But he was always a whole lot more than that. A three-time All-Pro and a five-time Pro Bowler, he was the athletic prototype of the 1960s offensive lineman, and there are few to this day who understand why he isn't in the Pro Football Hall of Fame though he has been on the ballot for decades.

More than that, he survived more than his share of injuries that would have kept most careers from starting. For example, at age 15 he was accidentally shot in the right arm with a shotgun and required four operations and skin grafts. Two years later, a nearly eight-inch-long piece of wood penetrated his groin and lodged near his spine while he was chasing a calf in a pasture.

In football, he chipped a vertebra in his neck, suffered a concussion and a detached retina, battled through torn ligaments in his ankle and, in 1964, missed the entire season when he underwent surgery on a tumor in his liver as well as surgery to have pieces of wood removed from his abdomen.

So this—in case there was any doubt—was one tough guy.

At the University of Idaho, Kramer had already established himself as a quality offensive lineman and, in those days when every player did what it took to help the cause, as a field goal kicker as well.

"I was second in the nation in field goals in 1957," Kramer said with a laugh. "With three."

Ironically it would be his ability to kick with that ungainly square-toed right shoe that would be the key to the most memorable game of his career.

Jerry Kramer. *Vernon J. Biever photo*

"I remember my last game at the University of Idaho, and it was a nasty day," he said. "It started Friday night, and it was rain before it turned to snow. And there were about 18 inches of snow on the ground before it turned back to rain. And we could only plow the field once, so it was just a swamp. And I know there were a few students at the game, but the paid attendance was one."

It was a far cry from what he would run into a few years later at Yankee Stadium.

Kramer recalled his rookie season with the Packers when he was called on to try a field goal in an exhibition game in Boston when it was no certainty at the time he would even make the team.

"I look up in the stands and there are like 45,000 people, there, and I'm just pissing in my pants, I'm so nervous," he said. "My right leg is shaking so bad that it's jumping up and down and I beat on it to try to stop it from shaking. So I kick the ball and it hits one of the offensive linemen right in the ass. The PA announcer says, 'The kick is blocked,' and I say, 'Thank you.'"

But Kramer found his spot with the Packers and soon became one of the irreplaceable figures on an offensive line that was almost as famous as the guys who ran and threw and caught the ball.

THE SETTING

The Giants were mad. The Giants were embarrassed. And the Giants wanted revenge after the 37-0 whipping the Packers had put on them the year before in Green Bay.

That day, the changing of the guard had officially begun in the NFL. The old-school dominance of the New York Giants was ending, and the Packers were emerging as the long dormant power now ready to rise again.

Now it was time for the sweet rematch and merciful redemption. But this time it was in Yankee Stadium, in front of their own fans, and the Giants knew—as veteran teams usually do—that this might be the surge of greatness for this team.

Nonetheless, the Packers went in as seven-point favorites and the weather report suggested it might snow and then turn to rain.

There was nothing said of the biting, swirling wind that would sweep into the stadium and make it almost impossible to play.

The Giants were led by the aerial acrobatics of Y.A. Tittle, who had set a league record that year with 33 touchdown passes. And Lombardi, again playing the mind games he was so proficient at, extolled the wonders of the Giants and insisted this team was much better than the one the Packers had crushed the year before.

"They have a better offensive line," Lombardi said at the time, and Giants coach Allie Sherman insisted his team was better because Tittle had a second year in the offense to learn his teammates and the plays better.

The Packers, of course, were the Packers. They would do what they always did, and that meant a healthy dose of fullback Jim Taylor, just enough of Bart Starr's passing and the great defense that always seemed to come through when it had to.

The question, though, was the kicking game. Paul Hornung, despite Lombardi's claims to the contrary, stood no chance of playing due to a knee injury. That meant Kramer would do the field goal kicking and defensive back Willie Wood would handle the kickoffs.

And in a game between evenly matched opponents like this, the kicking game likely would make the difference. It's something Jerry Kramer knew all too well.

Back then, kicking was still just a job and not a specialty as it is today. Soccer-style kickers? They played soccer and stayed away from football. At that time, the kicking chores were often handled by someone from the offense who kicked straight on and wore one of those square-toed shoes that looked like something from the Spanish Inquisition.

But Kramer enjoyed it, and when the opportunity came, he was no longer the skittery rookie he'd been in that preseason game in Boston. He was a now a seasoned NFL player who knew what his job entailed.

And the Packers would need him more than they ever thought.

THE GAME OF MY LIFE
By Jerry Kramer

I had a little burden on me that day because I was doing the kicking. Paul Hornung had been injured and wasn't able to play, and I was the backup field goal kicker. It was bitter day, bitter cold and I think with the wind it was very comparable to the cold of the Ice Bowl.

The wind was so ferocious in Yankee Stadium that I remember they had those old wooden benches on the sidelines that looked like something from a high school locker room. They were really small and quite ancient. The wind was blowing so hard that it actually blew the benches over at halftime and blew them onto the field, maybe 10 yards from the sidelines and onto the playing field. It was obviously a hell of a day to be trying to kick field goals.

Now walking into Yankee Stadium is a hell of a thrill. Walking in it with all those ghosts is another elevation of that. To be on the field and playing is an incredible experience. It was just awesome to be there.

We were going to try a field goal fairly early on. And there's Ed Katcavage and Andy Robustelli and Rosie Grier and Sam Huff is breathing heavily, and I'm saying to myself, "What in the world are you doing being on the same field with these greats?" I must have taken a wrong turn somewhere.

But I was not only awed by the moment and the stadium, but I was awed to be on the field with those great players. By then I had more experience, so I was able to keep my wits about me.

I ended up kicking three field goals and we won the game. We had beaten the Giants quite soundly the previous year for the championship, so it was a different story in their back yard. It was a hell of a football game. They blocked a punt somewhere in the first half, and we scored and kicked a couple of field goals along the way. So with two and a half minutes left to go, they hadn't scored again and if we could make a field goal, it looked like we could win the game. I knew if I made the last field goal, then we would win the game.

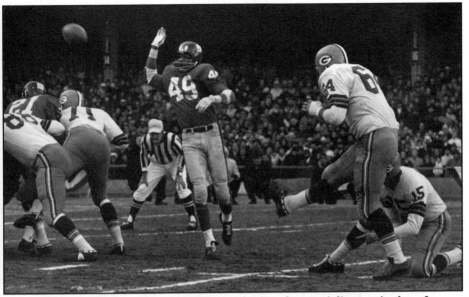

Jerry Kramer's three field goals in the swirling winds of Yankee Stadium were the key to the Packers' 1962 NFL title over the New York Giants. *Vernon J. Biever photo*

The wind was howling and carrying on, and I was kicking the ball outside the left upright and the wind carried it through the middle. It was a wonderful moment. It was a moment that running backs and quarterbacks have when you actually win a football game. I didn't feel that way in the Ice Bowl. That was supposed to be what you were out there for. I knew I had to make that block in the Ice Bowl and there was pressure. But it just didn't seem as much pressure as that Giants game.

It was a sensational moment and the team voted me the game ball. The funny thing is that the sports writers voted [linebacker Ray] Nitschke the game Corvette, and I got the game ball. Things always stay the same on the offensive line.

GAME RESULT

More than any game he ever played with the Packers, that one stood out for Jerry Kramer. He was the focal point of one of the most famous plays in football history, Bart Starr's quarterback sneak in the "Ice Bowl" in 1967. After all, he threw the key block that sprung Starr and put that game in the hall of the immortals.

"I think that whole final drive in the Ice Bowl was such a magnificent event that I really think of that game in terms of that [final] drive than in terms of the quarterback sneak," Kramer said. "I felt better in the Giants game because of the pressure of the moment."

Indeed, Kramer's three field goals from 26, 29 and 30 yards were all huge, but none was more important than the final 30-yarder with just two minutes to play. That's because if Kramer nailed it, it would give the Packers a nine-point lead and all but ensure, especially in those weather conditions, that New York could not make some miracle comeback.

All season Kramer's teammates had made fun of his rather unorthodox kicking style.

"I had a tendency to follow through very short," he said. "I was quite stiff in the joints because I was just a grunt in the middle of the pile. But my follow-through was a bit short, and the guys would really get on me in the locker room. They'd say, 'Sports quiz! Who is this?' and then they'd do a follow-through of about eight inches. They'd jack me around pretty good."

But on this frigid day and with everything on the line, there was no joking around. And that became clear when Kramer stepped into the huddle prior to the kick.

Several teammates looked at him somberly and said, "This is the ballgame, Jerry." Fellow guard Fuzzy Thurston said simply, "Keep your head down, buddy."

He did just that and, short follow-through and all, he drilled it through the uprights for the field goal that sealed the win.

"You didn't really think about it at the time," he said, though he remembers vividly being mobbed by his teammates as well as the heartfelt, solid handshake from Lombardi. "The biggest was it would have been nice to come off the field and catch your breath. I had to do a lot of running."

WHAT BECAME OF JERRY KRAMER?

Unlike many players who leave the game with no idea of what to do once the game didn't need them anymore, Kramer was lucky. Sort of.

In June of 1967, he began a daily diary of life in the NFL that became the book *Instant Replay*. Written with New York sports writer Dick Schaap, who became a lifelong friend after that, the book looked into the NFL the way no book had ever done before, and it was an instant success when it was published in 1968.

That was also the same year he retired from football, a shimmering part of five world championship teams including the first two games of what would be known as the Super Bowl. A year later, he wrote *Farewell to Football*, his ode to the game that had treated him so well.

He was the editor of a third book, *Lombardi: Winning is the Only Thing* in 1970 and in 1984, after a reunion of the Packers who won the first Super Bowl, he wrote *Distant Replay*, again with Schaap's help.

"I thought there might be something to say there, and there was," he said. "I visited with several of the guys, and it was a huge emotional experience."

What proved to be so emotional was the hold their old coach still had on many, if not all, of the players who had sweated and bled and worked for him. It was nearly 15 years after Lombardi's death, and the man and his influence still hung over them like a shadow.

"I knew it had been a powerful influence on my life and the other guys, but I didn't realize how strong it was until [that reunion]," Kramer said. "Just about every guy from Super Bowl I was at a crossroads in his life. For example, Lee Roy Caffey [a linebacker from 1964-69] had a bank charter down in Texas that he tried to get four or five different times. But they'd turned him down every time. Lee Roy's partners were getting discouraged and wanted to quit and he said to them, 'You can quit, but I can't. If

Lombardi found out he'd kill me.'" When I saw the depth of that impact, it made me feel like there was still something to say. That's what really got me. I didn't expect that."

He has dabbled in writing on and off since, even working on a screenplay about Lombardi that first caught the attention of the late actor George C. Scott, who reveled in the thought of playing the old coach.

But it never came together back in the 1970s, though Kramer hasn't given up hope of one day getting a movie made about his coach. Asked if he thought a film about a coach dead nearly 35 years could still be relevant today, he said with a laugh, "What do you think?"

And who would he pick to play Lombardi these days? Without hesitation he said Jack Nicholson.

Kramer was also involved in a nutrition business that went bankrupt.

"I'm trying to figure out what to do now," he said.

Mostly, though, he's made a nice career out of being a former Packer from the glory years, and he has been a popular speaker nationally who will go anywhere to talk about the team he loves.

"I have tried to retire several times," he said. "And I don't seem to be very good at it."

CHAPTER 6

LYNN DICKEY

"We could do anything we wanted."

Name: Clifford Lynn Dickey
Birthdate: October 19, 1949
Hometown: Paola, Kansas
Current residence: Leawood, Kansas
Position: Quarterback
Height: 6-4
Playing weight: 220
Years: 1976-85
College: Kansas State
Accomplishments: Two-time All Big-Eight quarterback...Led NFL in passing in 1983...Led Packers in passing for eight seasons...Third in team history in passes attempted (2,831) and completed (1,592) and in touchdown passes (133)...Still the team leader in most yards passing in a season (4,458 in 1983)...Inducted into Packer Hall of Fame in 1992.
The game: Washington Redskins, October 17, 1983 at Lambeau Field

THE LIFE OF LYNN DICKEY

Lynn Dickey is still the biggest thing to come out of Osawatomie High School. He was one of those once-in-a-lifetime high school hotshots who automatically made everybody better the minute he stepped on the field. And at Osawatomie, located 35 miles south of Kansas City in tiny Paola, Kansas, Clifford Lynn Dickey was about as good as anyone was going to see.

He proved it in 1966 when he led his high school to an unbeaten season and a state championship, and he gladdened the hearts of many Kansas residents when he decided to stay close to home and play football at Kansas State.

And it was more of the same in Manhattan, where in his career, Dickey passed for 6,208 yards and 29 touchdowns in three seasons. He still owns many of the significant passing records at K-State and finished his career by throwing for more than 380 yards four times, including a 439-yard strafing of Colorado in 1969. But the game that stays in the hearts of many longtime Kansas State fans also came in 1969, when he threw for 390 yards in a 59-21 pounding of Oklahoma in what remains the Sooners' worst loss ever.

Dickey was a two-time All-Big Eight Conference selection and was named Most Valuable Player of the East-West Shrine Game after his senior season. So impressive was his collegiate career that the Associated Press named him the greatest quarterback in Big Eight history and his No. 11 was the first retired by the university.

For Lynn Dickey, the road always seemed to be lined with success at every turn. And when he was taken by the Houston Oilers in the third round of the 1971 NFL draft, there seemed no reason to think anything would change. But the NFL, as too many college stars have found over the years, is a different animal from what they had experienced before.

The players are better, the game is faster, the expectations are constant and virtually unattainable, and the time you have to

Lynn Dickey. *Vernon J. Biever photo*

prove yourself is practically nonexistent. Dickey found that out in four rugged seasons with the Oilers. Injury and inconsistency dogged him all the time, and in four seasons he completed just 155 of 294 passes for 1,953 yards, eight touchdowns and a staggering 28 interceptions.

In today's NFL, those kinds of numbers would have sent a player into another line of work. But back then, there was at least a little more patience with players with the kind of intrinsic ability Dickey had.

And there was a team in desperate need of a quarterback that was ready to try to pull that potential out of Dickey, no matter what it took. The Green Bay Packers had struggled horrendously at quarterback ever since the immortal Bart Starr had retired after the 1971 season. And in April 1976, the Packers were ready to take a chance on another quarterback who might at least be able to reside in the same ballpark as Starr.

THE SETTING

It will go down, with little argument, as the worst trade in Packers history.

In 1974, the Packers inexplicably sent their first-, second- and third-round picks of the 1975 draft and their first and third selections in 1976 to the Los Angeles Rams for John Hadl, a quarterback who was already on the down slope of a career that hadn't been anything spectacular in the first place. But that's how desperate the Packers were for a quarterback.

Since Starr's retirement (and his subsequent assumption of the role as the team's offensive coordinator in 1972), the Packers were simply lost at the quarterback position. In 1972, Scott Hunter and Jerry Tagge combined to complete fewer than half of their passes with six touchdowns and nine interceptions. In 1973, Tagge Hunter and Jim Del Gaizo again could not get to the 50 percent completion mark and managed to combine for six touchdown passes and 17 interceptions. In 1974, Hadl, Tagge and the ancient Jack Concannon threw for five touchdowns and 21 interceptions, and in 1975, Hadl was horrific, throwing for 2,095 yards but with just six touchdowns and a mind-bending 21 interceptions.

After what the sainted Starr had done in his 16-year Hall of Fame career, it was practically sacrilege what those guys under center had done for the Packers. On top of that, by 1975 Starr had replaced Dan Devine as head coach, making the situation even more depressing.

So, barely a week before the NFL draft in 1976, the Packers decided to cut their losses and try to look toward the future. That's when they dealt Hadl, defensive back Ken Ellis, a fourth-round pick that year, and a third-rounder in 1977 to the Oilers for Lynn Dickey.

It seemed to be a trade that would work for everyone involved. Dickey, who had struggled with a hip injury the previous season, hadn't worked out in Houston and needed a change of scenery, and the Packers still needed a quarterback and wanted to put as much distance between themselves and John Hadl as possible.

There was no doubt this was another gamble with such a valuable position, but the Packers had almost no choice. And for a while, Dickey seemed to be the guy they needed that season. He played well enough, throwing for 1,465 yards and seven touchdowns (but also heaving up 14 interceptions) before suffering a separated shoulder against the Chicago Bears in the 10th week of the season and missing the rest of the year.

It got even worse in 1977 when Dickey continued to struggle, throwing 14 interceptions to just five touchdowns. Then in the ninth game of the season, Dickey severely broke his leg on the final play of the game against the Rams. The injury was so bad it forced him to miss the entire 1978 season. Still the Packers stuck with him.

In 1979, Dickey sat back as Whitehurst, who had started every game the previous season with decidedly mixed results (2,093 yards, 17 interceptions and 10 touchdowns in an 8-7-1 campaign that barely saw the Packers miss the playoffs) stayed in control. But by week 14, Starr had seen enough of mediocre quarterbacking.

He inserted Dickey for the final three weeks, and he completed 50 percent of his passes with five touchdowns and four interceptions, the first time since Starr himself in 1968 that a Green Bay quarterback had more touchdowns than picks. Then again, the Packers also lost two of those three games. But at least Starr believed he had a direction to go.

Things changed in the next two seasons, though, as Dickey became the clear leader on the offense; however, little changed on the scoreboard. In the next two years, Dickey threw for more than 6,000 yards and 32 touchdowns. But he also missed three more games due to injury in 1981, threw 40 interceptions, and the Packers went 13-18-1 on the field.

Bart Starr, who had shown so much faith and patience in Dickey, lost his duties as general manager after the 1980 season, but in 1981, he was rewarded with a two-year contract extension as head coach after Green Bay went 8-8 but still missed the play-offs.

Then in 1982, all the pain and suffering and heartache that accompanied this franchise seemed to finally be worth it. It was a season shortened to eight regular-season games by a vitriolic player's strike. It shut the league down for 57 days and ended up pitting player against player, coach against player and fan against player. It was one of those classic no-win situations that, not surprisingly, no one really won.

The NFL resumed play on November 21, and the Packers, who had been 2-0 when the strike began, finished with a solid 5-3-1 record that was good enough to get them into the postseason "tournament." Dickey certainly did his part to help, throwing for nearly 1,800 yards and 12 touchdowns.

The important thing was that the Packers, for the first time since 1972, were in the playoffs and, even more remarkable, they hosted a playoff game for the first time since the legendary "Ice Bowl" 15 years earlier.

In his postseason activity, Dickey was superb. In the opening-round game against the St. Louis Cardinals, he completed 17 of 23 passes for 260 yards and threw two touchdown passes to John Jefferson and one each to James Lofton and Eddie Lee Ivery in a thunderous 41-16 win.

In a second-round game at Texas Stadium against the Dallas Cowboys, he rang up 332 yards and a touchdown to Lofton, but he was also intercepted three times as Dallas advanced 37-26.

But these were the numbers the Packers had longed to see from a quarterback. Besides, the NFL was going through a less than subtle change on offense. Rules were opening up the game, and coaches—like San Diego's Don Coryell and San Francisco's Bill Walsh—were starting to use the passing game as more of a down-the-field weapon than anyone else before. Offense was becoming the name of the game, and Dickey and his Packers were becoming an integral part of it.

THE GAME OF MY LIFE
By Lynn Dickey

That Washington Redskins game was the most memorable only because the Redskins were coming off a season as defending Super Bowl champions. No one gave us much of a chance, and it was a Monday night game, so that was special, too.

In warmups for that game, it seemed the ball was just spinning. I can't explain it. Some days you can just tell in warmups that it's going to be a good day. And during the game I couldn't throw a wobbly pass if I tried. I was getting great protection and they were getting no rush on me whatsoever. It was like shooting fish in a barrel in the first half. Of course, we were having trouble stopping them too.

But I remember going back to Wednesday morning of that week—I forget who we played the week before—but the Redskins had seen the last three or four weeks' tape of the games we'd played. I think it was Redskins tight end Don Warren, though I wouldn't swear to it, who made a comment that made it back to our bulletin board in a hurry. He said that this game was going to be a rout. [Coach] Bart [Starr] got hold of that, and he didn't let things get under his skin often, but that did.

He put it up on the overhead projector that Wednesday and alluded to it every day after that. On the night of the game we went out for warmups and came back in, and before we were ready to come back out he put that quote back up on the overhead projector. He said, "This is what these guys think of you." He also said, "It's going to be a rout," but he added, "He didn't say which way," which we thought was kind of cool. It was a little extra pump for us.

It was just a fun game. You knew you were on Monday night television, and I think that game was the first one after the World Series had ended, so a lot of people were watching. Pretty much we could do whatever we wanted to do that night.

I don't remember the score at the half, but right toward the end of the third quarter, it was 35-34 or something and (offensive

Lynn Dickey played on some horrible Packers teams and never got the credit he deserved for being one of the NFL's most dangerous passers. *Vernon J. Biever photo*

coordinator) Bob Schnelker looked at me on the sidelines and elbowed me and said, "Keep plugging away. They can't stop us." He said we may have to score 40 points to win this game, and, looking back, we probably should have lost the game.

I remember Leotis Harris was hurt. He was the normal right guard, and Greg Koch was our normal right tackle. We just signed a new guy, Charlie Getty, and he played right guard. Koch and I were always arguing about something, and in the huddle during the game I saw Koch had his head down. His nickname was "Bubba," and I said, "Bubba, what's wrong?" And he said, "Man, I've got a headache." It turns out [Redskins mammoth defensive tackle] Dave Butz was head-butting him on every play, and Koch had this terrible headache.

I told him, "He's only got a one-yard jump on you, and he's getting a 10-yard jump on me. Just play your game." He said, "I'll do my job and you do yours." We argued like that in the huddle all the time. But Dave Butz didn't get to me the whole game.

I remember [left tackle] Karl Swanke got tangled up with [Washington star defensive end] Dexter Manley and he got into a scrap with Manley early in the game. He didn't get to me either. For the most part I had excellent protection.

There were a lot of ironies in the game, too. In Houston, I was the holder for Mark Moseley, and he kicked four field goals that night. He was a great kicker. He had lead in that right toe of his.

I remember at the end of the game after we kicked the field goal [to take a 48-47 lead], [Redskins quarterback] Joe Theismann did a wonderful job of leading them right back down the field and I'm thinking, "Oh my God, we scored 48 points and we're going to lose this thing." Joe had a great game, and we had a pretty good duel that night.

After the game, [Redskins fullback] John Riggins comes over to me and the first thing out his mouth is, "Some rout, huh?" It was just a crazy night. When you go to Lambeau Field you go there to have fun, and I think everybody had fun that night.

And it seems like every other year, it might be snowy outside and you can't get out of Kansas City, somebody will ask about the game and, since I have it on tape, I'll pop it in and look at it. I guess there will be a game like that again at some point. But at that time, when we weren't expected to do anything, it was a special night. Sometimes, when you least expect it, it will become a wild and crazy night.

GAME RESULT

Where to start? Early in that season, it was already obvious that the Packers were a phenomenal offensive machine. In the six games Green Bay had played prior to the Monday night orgy, it had already piled up 41 points against Houston, 27 against the Los Angeles Rams and 55 in a humiliation of the Tampa Bay Buccaneers.

Unfortunately for the offense, which could score from nearly anywhere on the field at any time, the Packers' defense had the same reputation. Anyone could score on that unit from anywhere at any time.

During those same six games, in fact, the defense surrendered 38 points to those same Oilers, 27 to the Giants, and 38 in an embarrassing loss to the Lions the week before. For the season, the Packers averaged 386 yards per game. The defense allowed an average of 400.

So it was no surprise to anyone that when the 5-1 Redskins steamed into Lambeau Field behind their formidable offense of Joe Theismann, John Riggins, Joe Washington, Charlie Brown, Art Monk and an offensive wizard like coach Joe Gibbs, no one gave the Packers much of a chance. The Redskins, coming off their first Super Bowl title, would go on to set an NFL record for most points in a season, but like the Packers, the defense had a tendency not to show up on occasion.

But the Packers, 3-3 and lucky to be that, figured they had very little to lose.

"We knew no one could really stop us on offense," center Larry McCarren recalled.

Ironically, it was the defense that set the tone in the game and provided the first points when linebacker Mike Douglass forced a Joe Washington fumble and returned it 22 yards for the touchdown barely a minute into the game. That was only the beginning.

Over the next 59 minutes, the two teams would wage the kind of war never before seen by Monday night football fans. Dickey completed 22 of 30 passes for 387 yards and three touchdowns and Theismann completed 27 of 39 passes for 398 yards and two scores.

The two teams combined for 95 points and 770 total yards, and by the time it was over, it took a shanked Mark Moseley field goal from 39 yards out to preserve Green Bay's 48-47 victory.

It was a game that remains the highest scoring in Monday night history and it remains a game that is as much a topic of conversation now as it was then.

WHAT BECAME OF LYNN DICKEY?

In 1983, Lynn Dickey enjoyed the kind of season most quarterbacks can barely even dream about it. That year, he set a club record by throwing for an astounding 4,458 yards as four receivers—Lofton, Jefferson, tight end Paul Coffman and running back Gerry Ellis—all caught at least 50 passes. Dickey also threw 32 touchdown passes but, as became part of the equation with him, 29 interceptions came along with them.

But he triggered one of the most fearsome offenses in the league, ringing up 6,172 total yards, second best in the entire NFL, and the 429 points were a team record until 1996. Unfortunately, the defense got no better and, in fact, was the NFL's worst, surrendering a ghastly 439 points, still a team record. Yet somehow, the Packers managed an 8-8 record.

But it was nowhere near good enough, and after nine seasons, one trip to playoffs, and a record of 53-77-3, Starr was fired as head coach and replaced by another legend from the golden era, former right tackle Forrest Gregg.

For Dickey the end was already in sight. Though he threw for 3,195 yards and 25 touchdowns in 1984, he became part of a three-quarterback merry-go-round in 1985 that also included Randy Wright and former Seattle Seahawk Jim Zorn. Dickey started 10 games and threw for just over 2,200 yards and 17 touchdowns as Green Bay went 8-8 for the second straight year.

His last start, though, was a memorable one. In a December 1 blizzard at Lambeau Field, he led the Packers' offense to 512 total yards in a 21-0 win over Tampa Bay. Later that week, though, while working out, Dickey injured his neck and never played again.

Once he left the game, Dickey toyed with the idea of coaching.

"But the main reason I didn't get into coaching was the commitment and the time," he said. "It was never really my type of commitment. If it was a nine-to-five job I'd do it, but it's not nine to five and it never will be."

Today he works in the automobile extended warranty business as a salesman and he gets up to Wisconsin frequently.

And even now, he remembers back to the incredible October night more than 20 years ago when everything fell into place.

"It's amazing," he said. "I could almost tell you everything that was going to happen in that game. I can still hear the audibles. It was really something."

CHAPTER 7

WILLIE DAVIS

"I'm not going to be denied."

Name: William Delford Davis
Birthdate: July 24, 1934
Hometown: Lisbon, Louisiana
Current residence: Inglewood, California
Position: Defensive end
Height: 6-3
Playing weight: 240
Years: 1960-69
College: Grambling State
Accomplishments: Inducted into Pro Football Hall of Fame in 1981...Five-time Pro Bowler and five-time All-Pro...Never missed a game in a 12-year career spanning 162 games...Holds all-time team record for recovered fumbles with 21...Inducted in Packer Hall of Fame in 1975.
The game: New York Giants, December 31, 1961 at City Stadium

THE LIFE OF WILLIE DAVIS

It's a story as old as football itself. Find a kid who loves football and chances are his mother won't want him to play. It's a maternal thing that runs deeper than the ocean—no mother wants to see her little baby get hurt, and football was the surest way to get a mom worrying.

Willie Davis's mom, Nodie, who raised Willie and his two siblings by herself, was the perfect example. The problem was, Willie Davis loved football and was a star at Booker T. Washington High School in Texarkana, Arkansas.

He recalls a story about how he never told his mother he was playing high school football. But the story fell apart the third week of the season when the team had to play a road game and Willie knew she'd find out because he'd be out so late.

Mom acquiesced and Willie flourished. He earned a football scholarship at Grambling University and was a two-year team captain and an NAIA All-American.

Though he harbored thoughts of playing professionally, he wasn't sure what chance he'd have playing for a small school like Grambling. He got his answer thanks to a 19-tackle performance in a late-season upset win over Florida A&M that a number of pro scouts were watching. He went on to become a 17th-round draft pick of the Cleveland Browns in 1956, though his career was put on hold due to army service in 1956-57.

He came out of the service and back to the Browns, but the team had trouble finding a position for him. First on the offensive line and then to the defensive line and back again, coach Paul Brown was uncertain what to do with him. And the frustration on both sides was growing.

That's when the fateful decision was made that would alter the future of Willie Davis and the Green Bay Packers.

Willie Davis. *Vernon J. Biever photo*

THE SETTING

Even today Davis wonders what might have happened if he hadn't ended up with the Packers. He runs it through his mind and wonders what would have happened if the Browns had showed infinite patience and kept him. Or worse, what if they had thrown up their hands and released him? What would have happened to him then?

"Coming to Green Bay was the best thing that ever happened to me," he said.

But that's hardly how he felt at the time when, prior to the 1960 season, frustrated at his inability to find a real position for Davis, Brown dealt him to the Packers for end A.D. Williams. No one is quite sure what happened to A.D. Williams, who had played the 1959 season in Green Bay and caught one pass for 11 yards. Few have to ask whatever happened to Willie Davis.

At the time, though, Davis was shocked by the thunderbolt out of nowhere and briefly considered quitting football altogether rather than play in the NFL hinterland like Green Bay.

But he would get the chance to *play* in Green Bay, something that was never a sure thing in Cleveland. Coach Vince Lombardi loved Davis's size and quickness and saw him as the prototypical defensive end.

"I consider speed, agility and size to be the three most important attributes for a defensive lineman," Lombardi told Davis at the time. "Give me a man who has any two of those dimensions and he'll do OK. But give him all three and he'll be great. We think you have all three."

That's all Davis needed to hear. He settled in at left end and for the next decade never left.

After coming up short in the NFL title game in 1960 against the Eagles, the Packers were back in 1961, looking for their first title since 1944.

THE GAME OF MY LIFE
By Willie Davis

Championship games will always highlight your memory more than anything, even though they may not have been your best game in terms of individual performances. I remember the championships as if they were yesterday and remember the plays even as they occurred. The 1961 championship game in Green Bay against the Giants was one of the best total performances I'd ever seen. We beat them 37-0.

I think it was so memorable because of what it meant for us that we had not been able to achieve the year before against the Eagles [a 17-13 championship loss in Philadelphia]. Much of what emanated from that Eagles game was what Vince Lombardi told us. He said after that game that we would never lose another championship game as long as he was coaching. That was pretty strong talk. That's why I think we went out and decimated the Giants. The offense, the defense, everybody played at a level that, in my mind, was one of our best performances.

Add to that the fact that it was played in Green Bay and it was the first championship in a long, long time. It had all the things that would cause you to remember it for a long, long time. When we won the second championship [in 1962], it was important, but it was played in New York and it was just about the coldest game I ever played in.

But the 1961 game, I remember it was a cold Wisconsin day. It was nothing like the "Ice Bowl," but it was cold. It was the kind of day that Lombardi would often characterize as "our kind of day." And it was. It was cold, but you could play comfortably. It was a good day.

I was talking to Forrest Gregg just a few weeks ago and he was saying he had been able to get a complete copy of the 1961 game. I told him I needed to get one too, and he said, "I can see why, because they called your name a lot [on the public address]." It was one of my better games. I was playing [Giants] right tackle Jack Stroud, and I just remember every time they threw the ball we got pressure on the ball. It was strictly attitude. I said, "I'm not going to be denied today." It was a game built around confidence.

And as we dominated the game, the fans really got into it. I would say it was a love affair that day. It was something I don't think happened in any other game, because I remember them yelling out "Go get 'em, Willie." They were having a ball.

It was the greatest memory I had in football and it had to compare to my being traded from Cleveland to Green Bay and believing for a minute that Green Bay was the worst place in the NFL. [Browns coach] Paul Brown used to describe Green Bay as the Siberia of football. But it was the greatest 10 years of my life."

GAME RESULT

It was difficult for some Packers fans to remember, but playing for the championship used to be commonplace in Green Bay. From 1929 through 1944, the Packers won six championships and became perhaps the first truly great franchise in a league still searching for its place in America.

On December 17, 1944, the Packers beat the New York Giants 14-7 for another title, and there seemed no end in sight to what the Packers could do.

But it did end—thunderously and quickly. In 1945, the Packers went 6-4 and by 1948 there was a losing season, and eight more would follow over the next decade. That's what made 1961 so special.

And when the Packers took the field against the Giants on that cold day, it was the first playoff game played in Green Bay since that championship game in 1944.

The Packers made it one to remember, too. After a scoreless first quarter, the Packers buried the Giants under 24 second-quarter points, led by Paul Hornung, who was playing on leave from the army. He scored on a six-yard run to start the scoring, and after Ray Nitschke and Hank Gremminger interceptions, Bart Starr threw touchdown passes to Boyd Dowler and Ron Kramer. Hornung ended that barrage with a 17-yard field goal and a 24-0 lead.

It was already over.

The Packers' defense, led by Davis and Nitschke, held the Giants to six first downs and 240 total yards, including just 31 rushing. The Packers also forced five turnovers, four interceptions and a fumble, and the defense chalked up the first NFL title game shutout in 12 years. Offensively, the Packers finished with 345 yards and Hornung was the star. Rushing for 89 yards, with his 19-yard field goal in the quarter, he set an NFL championship scoring mark of 19 points.

"This is the greatest team in the history of the National Football League," Lombardi proclaimed at the time.

He hadn't seen anything yet.

And Willie Davis was a massive part of it. For most of the 1960s, Davis was the preeminent defensive end in the NFL and all he knew, it seemed, were championships. From 1960 to 1967, he played in seven NFL championship games and was on the winning side six times—including in the first two of those games they would come to call the Super Bowl.

He would become a part of myth and lore and legend along with his Packers teammates and, collectively, their names would be uttered with a kind of reverence unknown to pro sports up to that point.

But these were not marble men. They were not statues who needed only to spend their days adjusting themselves on their pedestals. They were flesh and blood humans who bled and cried and were wracked by the doubts that haunted everyone else. And Willie Davis was no different.

He remembers only too well the first NFL-AFL championship game in January, 1967. In past years, these Packers at least knew what to expect. They knew what stood in front of them and they could deal with it, because familiarity, if it didn't breed confidence, at least led to an understanding of what the job was.

But on this day, the Packers were facing the Kansas City Chiefs. The Kansas City Chiefs? These were not the Dallas Cowboys or the Cleveland Browns or New York Giants—real teams from the only league that the Packers figured mattered.

But the football world was changing. The established NFL and the upstart AFL were merging into one league and the necessary result was that the best of the NFL had to play the AFL's champ, and that meant that the Packers were at center stage.

And the Packers knew, as did coach Vince Lombardi, that this was a no-win situation for the NFL. Win the game and it was what was expected. Lose? Oh my God, the thought was too awful to contemplate. Willie Davis understood that with every other Packer.

"I'm lying in bed the night before the game and I'm wide awake," Davis said. "I'm asking myself what concerns me most personally and what concerns me about the team. I answered my concerns about me. There was a lot of confidence, but I had to be careful not to make the big mistake. I didn't want to make the mistake that would cost us the game. Our whole philosophy at Green Bay was that on defense we had to make a team earn every touchdown. And we had to do it by making the other team travel the length of the field to do it. And if you made a team run that many plays, there was always something that seemed to happen to upset that continuity. We wanted to make sure that happened again."

Lombardi also stressed to his team not to take the Chiefs lightly.

"He'd say, 'Look at their roster, it's full of the top college players from the last five years. You've got to know these guys have an excellent chance to be a good football team against you.'"

He never said, however, that the Chiefs had a chance to beat the Packers. Lombardi would never say something like that. And there was more a sense of relief than true joy after the Packers' 35-10 win. It was much the same the next year when the Packers pounded the Oakland Raiders.

And while the Packers had put their names among the NFL's best of all time, even they knew it could not last.

WHAT BECAME OF WILLIE DAVIS?

By 1969, Willie Davis knew the end had come not only for himself but the golden years of the Green Bay Packers. The players who had made up the backbone of those incredible teams were either retiring or being traded.

Lombardi left the sidelines for one uncomfortable season as general manager in 1968. Max McGee, Fuzzy Thurston and Don Chandler retired while Jerry Kramer, Ray Nitschke, Henry Jordan, Forrest Gregg, Willie Wood and Davis were all heading in that direction. The dynasty was ending. Davis played through the 1969 season and decided his time had come as well.

It is a common and sad story about how players leave pro sports and are ill equipped to handle the real world that follows. But Willie Davis didn't fall into that trap.

Actually, he learned a valuable lesson from his experience in Cleveland, realizing that one day you can be on a pro team and the next you could be history. He told himself even then that he was not going to be caught flat-footed when his football career ended.

He majored in industrial arts at Grambling and late in his career in Green Bay, he went after his master's degree in business from the University of Chicago. Once he retired, job offers came from the private sector as well as from football, where NFL teams thought he'd make a good assistant coach and several colleges thought he'd be a terrific head coach.

But Davis had his sights set on other things. He went into the Schlitz Brewing Company management program in 1967 and then in 1970 took over the Schlitz distributorship in Los Angeles. Since then he has become one of Southern California's most successful businessmen.

He serves on 10 corporate boards of directors including megapowers like Dow Chemical and Sara Lee Corp. He still maintains his ties in Wisconsin as well, serving on the boards of Johnson Controls Inc. and Wisconsin Energy Corp. He is president of All Pro Broadcasting, a radio chain with stations in Milwaukee and Los Angeles, which generates about $7 million in revenues.

These were plans that Davis set out to accomplish long ago. Driven first by his love of football, then by Lombardi and finally by his desire to be a success after football, Davis achieved nearly everything he set out to do. He says now he will scale back on his board of director duties and try to enjoy life a little more.

But he remains passionate about the Green Bay Packers. He never misses an opportunity to return for games and he will always be on hand for alumni functions. He was an early and strident backer of the Packers' original and controversial plan to renovate Lambeau Field to the tune of $295 million. And when the plans were first unveiled, Davis was there to offer full support.

He knows how fortunate he was to land in what, for him, was the perfect situation. And he made the most of it.

"I look at it and I realize I ended up playing for one of the greatest coaches ever and absolutely the greatest fans ever," he said. "And that's an enjoyment that still endures."

CHAPTER 8

KEN RUETTGERS

"It was as electric as it had ever been."

Name: Kenneth Francis Ruettgers
Birthdate: August 20, 1962
Hometown: Bakersfield, California
Current residence: Sisters, Oregon
Position: Left tackle
Height: 6-5
Playing weight: 285
Years: 1985-95
College: University of Southern California
Accomplishments: First-round draft choice of the Packers in 1985
The game: Pittsburgh Steelers, December 24, 1995 at Lambeau Field

THE LIFE OF KEN RUETTGERS

To understand a complicated guy like Ken Ruettgers is to try to understand the impossible. And in many ways that's exactly the way he wanted it.

This was not some mastodon-like offensive lineman who understood words of only two syllables or less. He was bright, well read, and opinionated and would just as soon talk about the politics of abortion or the role of the United Nations as he would about his blocking assignment that Sunday.

As well, this was an offensive lineman who was also a quality athlete. At Garces High School in Bakersfield, he was certainly a star in football as both an offensive tackle and defensive end. But he also played basketball, threw the shot and discus and even lettered in golf.

He was good enough to earn a scholarship at Southern Cal and, after two years as a backup guard, he was moved to tackle, where he thrived. Unfortunately, he was also getting an early taste of the injury bug that would plague him most of his NFL career and that would lead to one of the great disappointments in his football career. He missed all of his 1980 season with a broken hand and knee injury.

But by the time he was through playing at USC, and earning his B.S. in business administration, he had developed a reputation as a solid, steady left tackle. And the Packers noticed.

The left tackle position remains the most vital on the offensive line, because that's where the most damage can be done by a defense. Using the theory that most quarterbacks are right-handed, when they drop back to throw, their blind side is to the left. Consequently that's where most defenses put their best pass rusher, because a great rush at a quarterback who can't see him coming is usually the recipe for mayhem. So the offensive line is made and broken by how well the left tackle plays.

The Packers liked Ruettgers so much coming out of college that on draft day in 1985, they gave up the 14th pick overall to the

Ken Ruettgers. *Tom G. Lynn/Time Life Pictures/Getty Images*

Buffalo Bills for the Bills' seventh pick and a second-round selection just so they could move up to get Ruettgers.

It proved to be an inspired move as Ruettgers would play in all 16 games as a rookie and start twice. By the next season, he had moved in as the starting left tackle, and for the next decade he rarely budged for anything except injury.

THE SETTING

This was new territory for Ken Ruettgers, who in 10 years of toiling in virtual anonymity on the Packers' offensive line had been a part of exactly four winning seasons and had yet to see anything resembling a playoff game.

He had played for former Packers legends like Forrest Gregg in the early years, and then Lindy Infante took over in 1988 and seemed to have the team poised to do great things, especially after a 10-6 performance in 1989 that left the Packers just short of the playoffs.

But they fell back again the next two years, and Mike Holmgren, Ruettgers's third head coach, took over. He too seemed like he had the Packers going where they needed to go with 9-7 records three straight years and playoff appearances in 1993 and 1994. But it was time for the next step, wasn't it?

The Packers had proven they could reach the playoffs, but both times it had been as a wild card and life as an NFL wild card is rarely a pleasant experience. They needed a division title and the chance to prove that they had truly arrived. And 1995 looked to be the season when that would happen.

All the pieces were in place. There was a young, charismatic quarterback named Brett Favre who could throw footballs where no one else even dreamed of throwing them. He threw to an up-and-coming wider receiver named Robert Brooks and a burly tight end named Mark Chmura, and Edgar Bennett was a young talented back.

On defense, Reggie White had put the Packers on the map, veteran Sean Jones provided a fearsome bookend to White, and

Leroy Butler was developing into one of the NFL's best safeties. So it was all there for the taking.

But by midseason, the Packers were still nothing more than an average team. After a disastrous loss to the Minnesota Vikings in the Metrodome in which Favre and backup quarterback Ty Detmer were both knocked out of the game with injuries, Green Bay stood at a pedestrian 5-4.

Then came the turning point of the season. Favre had badly sprained his ankle against the Vikings, and few figured he'd play the following Sunday in a huge matchup with the Chicago Bears. Detmer had already been ruled out of the game with a thumb injury, and the Packers were so desperate for a healthy quarterback that Holmgren lured a friend and protégé from the San Francisco 49ers, Bob Gagliano, out of retirement to take snaps just in case.

But Favre knew what no one else did. Around-the-clock treatments on the ankle and a plan to tape it so tight that it would essentially be a cast would allow him to play. And he knew it.

Favre then produced a game that Packers fans still remember with awe. Hobbling around on the ankle, he completed 25 of 33 passes for 336 yards, five touchdowns and no interceptions as the Packers beat the Bears.

From there, the Packers took off, winning five of six, including a 34-23 win in New Orleans on December 16 that secured another playoff spot. But another playoff spot isn't all the Packers were looking for. With a win over Pittsburgh the following week, Green Bay could wrap up its first NFC Central Division title since 1972.

It was there for the taking.

THE GAME OF MY LIFE
By Ken Ruettgers

It was the last game of the season and it was right around Christmas. We needed a win to win the division and to get home field advantage in the playoffs. And it was one of those typical slugfests. The Packers were a very physical team at Lambeau

Field and Pittsburgh, of course, was a very physical team. It was just one of those games that went back and forth for the whole game. It was really something.

Both teams really went back and forth and right at the end, the Steelers drove down and [wide receiver] Yancey Thigpen was wide open in the end zone for the winning touchdown. I'm on the sideline and I remember thinking, "This is it, this is the whole season." [Quarterback] Neil O'Donnell went on play action and Thigpen was all alone and I went, "Oh man." Even from the sidelines watching it, it looked like it was in slow motion. And then he dropped the ball. I couldn't believe it.

The crowd and the atmosphere and the lights were on and it was just an unbelievable scene. We took over [for the final few snaps] and there's Brett in the huddle and Robert Brooks is smiling. I remember a Beatles song came on the PA and Brooks started doing an air guitar. It was as electric as it had ever been in Lambeau since I'd been there in 11 years. I remember going into the locker room after the game, and I'm not a very expressive celebratory person, but it was a sweet moment. [Team president] Bob Harlan and I had invited Rush Limbaugh to the game, and we all celebrated with a cigar.

I remember we had hats made that said "NFC Central Division Champs." I'm glad we didn't have to burn them. It was a big step.

There were other great games like the Bears and Packers, but this one was the march toward the Super Bowl that had to be made. This started it all.

GAME RESULT

Even today, no one really understands how Yancey Thigpen dropped a pass that could not have been placed in his arms any better. But it happened, and all the sheepish Thigpen, a Pro Bowl wide receiver, could say was "Merry Christmas, Green Bay."

The Packers could have won the division the easy way by getting some help from Tampa Bay in its season finale against Detroit.

In perhaps the ultimate irony, after 11 years with the Packers, Ken Ruettgers retired in the middle of the 1996 season, two months before the Packers won the Super Bowl. *Vernon J. Biever photo*

But the Buccaneers couldn't come through, losing to the Lions 37-10. That meant the Packers would have to take the division by force.

Green Bay led 14-10 at halftime and built its advantage to 21-13 after three quarters and setting up the final dramatics.

Early in the fourth quarter, the Packers were driving for another score when Favre was clobbered by unblocked Steelers linebacker Kevin Greene. Favre, who had been smacked around all day by the swarming Steelers defense, was truly shaken up after this one. He stood up, then went to a knee and began spitting up blood. According to Ruettgers, the blood came from Favre biting his tongue during the hit, but it looked far more sinister than that. Whatever it was, it forced him out for the rest of the series and the Packers had to settle for a Chris Jacke field goal and 24-13 lead.

Pittsburgh roared back and scored a touchdown, though it missed the crucial two-point conversion that could have made all the difference.

When the Packers couldn't move on their next possession, Pittsburgh quarterback Neil O'Donnell methodically drove the Steelers toward another score, a Steelers win and more heartache for the Packers.

But deep in Packers territory, the drive stalled, and on fourth down with 11 seconds to play, O'Donnell rolled and looked for Thigpen, who was wide open in the left corner of the end zone after he beat Packers cornerback Lenny McGill.

O'Donnell lofted the ball so gently and so effortlessly that the air came out of the stadium. It was over. And then Thigpen simply dropped the ball, setting off a huge celebration on the Packers' sideline.

The Packers won 24-19, though Pittsburgh, which would end up losing to Dallas in Super Bowl XXX, dominated much of the game. The Steelers had 398 total yards to Green Bay's 359 and held the edge in time of possession and first downs. Favre threw for 301 yards and Robert Brooks had a huge game with 11 receptions for 137 yards.

WHAT BECAME OF KEN RUETTGERS?

Players never know when the end is staring them in the face. Then again, maybe they do and they just don't want to acknowledge its existence. Whatever it was for Ken Ruettgers, that game would end up being the highlight of his career. And probably somewhere deep down, Ruettgers knew it.

The Packers went on to host a first-round playoff game and beat the Atlanta Falcons. Then they went to San Francisco and defied the odds one more time by shocking the powerful 49ers in Candlestick Park. That set up the NFC championship game in Dallas against a Cowboys team the Packers had lost to five straight times, including the last two years in the postseason.

And though the Packers led the Cowboys heading into the fourth quarter, two Dallas touchdowns sent the Packers home disappointed one more time.

The next step had been taken, but it still wasn't far enough.

But this was the end of line for Ruettgers. Plagued for several years by a chronic knee problem, he told the Packers that he might not be able to play in 1996.

The Packers pleaded with him to rehab the knee in the off season and try to play. But in the meantime, they drafted another USC left tackle, John Michels, with their first pick in the draft—just in case. They also signed a free agent, Bruce Wilkerson, who would pay massive dividends down the road.

The plan was for Ruettgers to play one more season and tutor the young Michels; then Ruettgers could slip away into pain-free retirement in 1997. But the plan never came together. Despite off-season surgery, a degenerative knee problem kept Ruettgers out of training camp and Michels was thrown into action immediately, even though he was far from ready.

Ruettgers started the season on the physically unable to perform list and by the time he was ready to come off at midseason, he knew he was through. On November 20, he announced his retirement and could only watch longingly as the Packers rolled to the Super Bowl title he had spent 11 long years striving for. Michels couldn't hold the job, and by the playoffs, Wilkerson had taken over.

As for Ruettgers, he swears there are no regrets.

"When you get off the plane and you can barely walk down the stairs, it just wasn't worth it," he said. "If it was doable, there might have been regrets. But I just couldn't do it."

Ruettgers segued seamlessly into life after football. He stayed in Green Bay with his wife, Sheryl, and three kids for the next year or so, coaching some football and figuring out what he wanted to do with the rest of his life. He went to work for a publishing company in Sisters, Oregon, and then formed a nonprofit company called "Games Over" to help former players transition to life after sports. He's also working toward his doctorate in philosophy.

"The Packers were such a big part of our lives," he said.

CHAPTER 9

MIKE DOUGLASS

"Everything fell together."

Name: Michael Reese Douglass
Birthdate: March 15, 1955
Hometown: Los Angeles, California
Current residence: Alpine, California
Position: Linebacker
Height: 6-0
Playing weight: 210
Years: 1978-85
College: San Diego State
Accomplishments: Packers fifth-round draft pick in 1985 …Played eight seasons in Green Bay and never missed a game…Named All-Pro in 1982 and 1983…Inducted into Packer Hall of Fame in 2003.
The game: Tampa Bay Buccaneers, October 2, 1983 at Lambeau Field

THE LIFE OF MIKE DOUGLASS

He isn't sure where the nickname came from or even who gave it to him, but it fit perfectly: Mad Dog. He was a linebacker's linebacker, with the mentality and physical gifts that made him one of the most consistent players around.

At San Diego State, he was a terror, posting a stunning 193 tackles and a staggering 32 quarterback sacks in his final two seasons for the Aztecs. His size was an issue, however, because even in the late 1970s, 200-pound linebackers weren't exactly what NFL teams were looking for.

Nonetheless, the Packers made Douglass one of their fifth-round draft picks in 1978, a draft that also produced James Lofton and John Anderson. And almost immediately, Douglass proved that size is only an issue if you don't have the heart.

He saw considerable playing time as a rookie, then moved in as the starting right linebacker in 1979 and did not leave for the next eight seasons.

In 1981, he finished with a career-high 146 tackles, the second most in club history, and he was tabbed by the state media as the Packers' Defensive Player of the Year.

THE SETTING

The Packers of 1983 were a study in schizophrenia that would have left any psychiatrist seeking treatment. They were fearsome on offense with weapons like Lofton, John Jefferson, Paul Coffman, Gerry Ellis and quarterback Lynn Dickey.

These Packers rang up 6,172 total yards, the second best total in the NFL behind the San Diego Chargers, and they scored 429 points, a franchise record that stood for 13 years.

But the defense was simply horrendous. Whether it was the scheme or the execution or just the personnel, for every point the offense scored, the defense seemed to give back two. Eight times opponents gained more than 400 yards on the Packers' defense,

Mike Douglass. *Vernon J. Biever photo*

and only twice all season did the defense hold teams under 20 points. For the season, the defense gave up a not-quite-believable 400 yards per game, the worst in the NFL and the most given up by any team in the league except for the 1981 Colts.

It was a team of wild fluctuations from game to game, from quarter to quarter and sometimes from play to play. Indeed, after that nearly perfect 55-14 win over Tampa Bay, the Packers went to Detroit the following week and were lathered by the Lions 38-14. The next week was the infamous and epic Monday night win over Washington followed by an overtime loss to Minnesota.

So it's not hard to understand how the Packers, who had an offense that was good enough to make the playoffs, staggered in with an 8-8 record and cost Bart Starr his job as head coach.

But even that season, with a defense that seemed practically helpless at time, Douglass did his fair share. He was named All-Pro that season after posting 127 tackles, forcing four fumbles, recovering four others and returning two of them for touchdowns. He also had five and a half quarterback sacks.

THE GAME OF MY LIFE
By Mike Douglass

It was against Tampa Bay in 1983 at home. I think it was the fact that it was during the time that Tampa was starting to get more recognition as a solid team and I remember they had beaten us badly in Tampa the year before [actually it was 1981 and Tampa won 37-3. Because of the strike in 1982, the two teams didn't play each other]. But this was the perfect day for football and the whole idea was to take them apart. I think we beat them 55-14, and it was a big win for us.

Defensively we were unstoppable. In that game I had a sack that turned into a fumble, and I ran it in for a 35-yard touchdown. Phillip Epps had an 80-yard punt return. The special teams did well, our defense was good, and the offense was dynamite. I think all the wide receivers caught at least four balls for us. It was just one of those days when everything fell together.

I remember that it had never been so loud in that stadium. I think the fans really kept up the juice and the excitement. They didn't give us a chance to come down. The crowd stayed in the game from the first whistle to the end. I remember walking through the parking lot before the game and it was crazy out there. I used to spend a lot of time in the parking lot after the game and after that one I knew that was the way football was supposed to be played. Our 12th man [the crowd] was definitely there.

Sometimes you think Packers fans are totally geared toward the game, but they were in tune. They were waiting for us to turn a corner. And those teams were always a lot of fun. We were just a man short here or there.

I watched almost every one of our offensive plays. I always wanted to see what was going on. James Lofton was my roommate, and John Jefferson I've known since San Diego State. These were

Mike Douglass (53), celebrating with cornerback Mark Lee, never missed a game in eight seasons with the Packers. *Vernon J. Biever photo*

guys you knew would be superstars, and you didn't want to miss a play.

GAME RESULTS

The Buccaneers never had a chance in this one. It was the Packers' offense operating at peak efficiency and the Packers playing the way they would not play the rest of the season. The combination was devastating.

And it began the very first time the Packers touched the ball when Phillip Epps returned a Bucs punt 90 yards for the game's first score. It continued on Green Bay's next possession when Dickey connected with Jessie Clark on a 75-yard touchdown pass.

Then it really got interesting.

In a record-setting second-quarter barrage, the Packers scored 35 points on a Harlan Huckaby touchdown run followed by another Dickey touchdown toss to tight end Paul Coffman.

Then Douglass got in on the fun, sacking Tampa Bay quarterback Jack Thompson and forcing a fumble. He gathered up the loose ball and ran 35 yards for the touchdown. Then fellow linebacker John Anderson joined the festivities by hauling back an interception 27 yards for a score. The onslaught ended when Dickey found James Lofton for a 57-yard scoring strike. The dust had settled and the Packers led 49-7—and even this defense wasn't going to let a lead like that slip away.

The 49 first-half points set an NFL record first established by the Packers in 1967 and showcased just about every weapon this remarkable offense had to offer.

For the game the Packers rolled up 519 yards, including 355 through the air and 164 rushing. Meanwhile the defense—which would suffer its share of indignities as the season continued—shimmered, holding the Buccaneers to 293 total yards and forcing three turnovers.

It was a humiliating performance by the winless Bucs, who just three years earlier had been a game away from going to the

Super Bowl. And afterward, a seething coach John McKay was in no mood to face anyone, especially the media.

When a reporter had barely gotten a word out of his mouth to ask the first question, McKay erupted, saying "Get the hell away from me before I punch you in the mouth."

With that he wheeled and walked out. After all, there really was nothing to say.

WHAT BECAME OF MIKE DOUGLASS?

In eight seasons, Mike Douglass never missed a game for the Green Bay Packers. Not once. Despite playing a jaw-rattling position like linebacker, and playing it at only 205 pounds, Douglass was the epitome of consistency, dedication and, perhaps, just a little good luck.

In those years, he led the Packers in tackles three times and even managed 11 interceptions. The capper came in his final season with the Packers in 1985 when he picked off a pass against Detroit and returned it 80 yards for a touchdown in a 26-23 win. But in his years, the Packers were always just a step behind no matter how much of an effort he put in. Still, he rarely showed any frustration.

To his credit, Douglass had always taken care of his body and knew that to handle the rigors of the NFL, he had to keep his body in top condition. He followed that creed from his earliest days in Green Bay and he still does it today.

He played for the Packers until 1985 and then played one season for the San Diego Chargers before deciding to give it up. From there, the next step was a logical one.

With his devotion to nutrition and keeping his body in perfect shape, he became a professional body builder and won dozens of competitions around the nation. But unlike many body builders who use steroids and other growth hormones to build mass, Douglass competed only in drug-free competitions.

Even today, nearly 20 years after leaving the game, he remains a physical specimen. He has opened a string of personal training and nutritional stores around California. His classes stress proper nutrition, and to that end most of his clubs have kitchens that hold cooking classes.

"I found the fountain of youth and I take it to the hilt," he said. "I don't even have any scars [from football] that make me remember playing. I definitely attribute that to how I live my life. It enabled me to recover after every game."

He remains close with many former teammates and he still has his fond memories of playing for the Packers, though he's one of the players who never enjoyed playing in the cold weather.

"I never adjusted to it," he said. "Forrest always felt that if you were going to play outside you should practice outside. Football is a mental state of mind and you adapt to the cold. And it was an advantage for us. You knew it could always get colder, and the other team starts thinking that it can get colder, too. So it did help us."

But in the long run, it didn't help all that much. In Douglass's eight seasons in Green Bay he saw two winning seasons and another four 8-8 seasons. He played in one playoff game, during the strike-shortened 1982 season.

Still, that didn't diminish his love of playing in Green Bay.

"I remember one day at practice this kid comes up to me for an autograph and I was baffled," he said. "We weren't doing that good, but he still wanted my autograph. I asked him why, and he said, 'Dude, you guys are the Green Bay Packers.' That put it in my mind that this was a unique organization. It was nice to be part of that whole development."

CHAPTER 10

RON KRAMER

"It was a complete pleasure to beat the Bears."

Name: Ronald John Kramer
Birthdate: June 24, 1935
Hometown: Girard, Kansas
Current residence: Fenton, Michigan
Position: Tight end
Height: 6-3
Playing weight: 230
Years: 1957-64
College: University of Michigan
Accomplishments: Named All-Pro in 1962 and 1963...Named to Pro Bowl in 1962...Inducted into Packers Hall of Fame in 1975...All-America tight end at Michigan.
The game: Chicago Bears, September 29, 1957 at City Stadium

THE LIFE OF RON KRAMER

There was almost nothing Ron Kramer couldn't do when it came to athletics. Born in Kansas, he moved to Detroit and eventually the University of Michigan, where he earned nine letters—three each in football, basketball and track.

In basketball, he set Michigan's all-time scoring record with 1,124 points, a mark that stood until 1961. On the track team, he was a gifted high jumper. But it was in football where Kramer really flourished.

He was a superb receiver and a good punter and placekicker, and when the occasion called for it, he could run the ball as well. In three seasons with the Wolverines, Kramer caught 53 passes for 880 yards and nine scores, and he averaged 41 yards on his punts.

The Green Bay Packers, who were in the midst of a 12-year funk, knew they could use all the help they could get, so after taking Hornung, the Heisman Trophy winner from Notre Dame, with their bonus pick, they selected Kramer with the fourth pick in the 1957 draft. Kramer and Hornung would become infamous buddies and closer than brothers in many respects.

"I'd always get into his tree about being the MVP [of the college All-Star game]," Kramer said. "We still talk two or three times a week."

Kramer made an immediate impact on a Packers team desperate for any kind of playmakers, and he ended up catching 28 passes his rookie season before wrecking his knee in the final game of the season.

THE SETTING

There was City Stadium and then there was City Stadium. The first park by that name was built behind the new East High School and served as the Packers' home from 1925 to 1956. By the end of that tenure, though, the old stadium was more pre-Colombian art than anything resembling a modern stadium of the day.

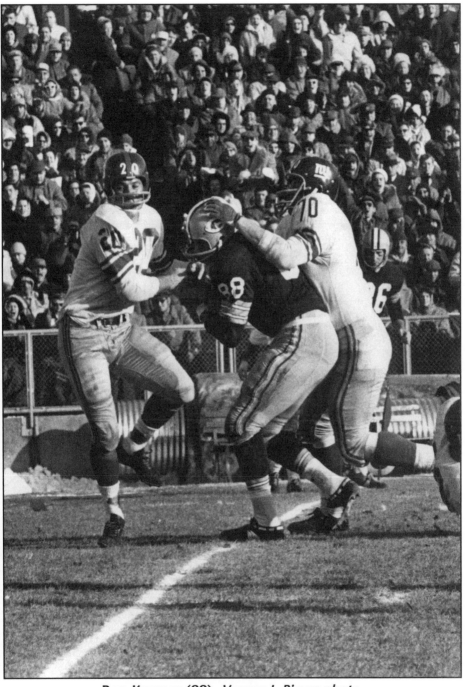

Ron Kramer (88). *Vernon J. Biever photo*

Knowing a new stadium was needed if the Packers wanted to stay viable, the residents of Green Bay passed a referendum in April of 1956, and the new City Stadium was built for the princely sum of $960,000. It seated 32,500 and featured the same bowl shape that it still has today despite a $295 million renovation.

In 1957, however, while the Packers remained wildly popular, their efforts on the field left much to be desired. The team hadn't won a championship since 1944, and three coaches—the legendary Curly Lambeau, Gene Ronzani and now Blackbourn—hadn't been able to re-create the magic. Indeed, in that period, Green Bay enjoyed just three winning seasons, and it would get worse before it got better.

Still, on a gorgeous fall afternoon, the Packers opened their new stadium. It was a day of pageantry and spectacle, featuring a parade as well as the appearances of vice president Richard Nixon, Miss America Marilyn Van Derbur, NFL commissioner Bert Bell, and biggest of all, actor James Arness, who played Marshall Matt Dillon in the popular TV show *Gunsmoke*.

And there was no better opponent for the Packers to face in the first game of their new digs than the hated Bears, who had clobbered the Packers twice the year before and whom the Packers had beaten just once in the previous four years.

THE GAME OF MY LIFE
By Ron Kramer

Everybody wants to put it in their minds that the most important games were championship games. I was drafted into Green Bay, into this little town, and they played in this stadium that seated 22,000 people. I went to the University of Michigan where we had 100,000 seats, so when I got here I said, "What's going on?" It sort of boggled my mind. I didn't know if I wanted to come up here. But they drafted me and they said you can make $20,000, and I said that's a hell of a deal to do what I wanted to do.

I went to Michigan because I wanted to be in business, and I decided through [Michigan coach] Fritz Crisler that I was going to try to do what Crisler told me. That's when I met Paul Hornung and we played in an All-Star game together and drove up to Green Bay in his 1948 or '49 Ford from Chicago.

So we get up here and we go through training camp with [coach] Lisle Blackbourn and the veterans suddenly decide they like us. Then it's our first game and it's the Chicago Bears, and everybody hated the Bears.

But there were 32,500 people there, and you would have thought we were playing for the world championship. I remember Richard Nixon was there and he was very gracious. He was everywhere, and it was like one of those times in my life where it was more important than a championship. It's what everybody dreams about. We beat the Bears, and that's what made that game important.

I remember everybody who played had a great game. It was just one of those days. It was opening day and it was a new stadium. We went on to win just two more games that season, but we beat the Bears. It was sort of neat.

It was such an absolute and complete pleasure to beat the Bears in the first game I ever played in. And you know what? I still don't care for them.

GAME RESULT

It was as true then as it is now when it comes to the Packers-Bears rivalry. The Packers could lose every game in a season, but if they beat only the Bears, then the season wasn't a total loss. And the Bears felt exactly the same.

In 1957, the Packers were still searching for a way out of the abyss. Bart Starr and Forrest Gregg had shown up the year before, but Jim Taylor, Jerry Kramer, Ray Nitschke, Herb Adderley and Dave Robinson hadn't arrived yet. No one knew about an obscure line coach for the New York Giants named Vince Lombardi, and the concept of "Titletown" was unknown.

All these Packers had to fight for was right there in front of them. Win a game, build some momentum and hope it continued. But it wasn't easy, and it hadn't been for a long time.

And while the Packers were coming off a pallid 4-8 season, optimism burned bright because there was a chance to start fresh, and why not start it against the Bears?

It began, and ended for that matter, just like a typical Bears-Packers brawl. Chicago scored the first points in the new stadium when quarterback Ed Brown ran in for a touchdown from five yards out. But the Packers came right back to tie it when backup quarterback Babe Parilli, subbing for the injured Starr, threw 37 yards to Billy Howton.

The Bears went back up on a Brown-to-Harlon Hill touchdown pass, and the Packers answered back with a one-yard touchdown run by fullback Fred Cone to tie the game at halftime.

The only scoring in the third quarter was a 13-yard George Blanda field goal for the Bears, though the Packers had their opportunities to score, too. The rookie Paul Hornung, however, missed two long field goal attempts. That set up the drama of the fourth quarter.

After the Packers' defense stopped the Bears on fourth down, Parilli came right back and connected with Howton on a 41-yard pass to the Bears' eight. Two plays later, Parilli eluded a strong pass rush, faded to his right and found tight end Gary Knafelc on his knees deep in the end zone for the touchdown and a Packers lead.

Chicago still had eight minutes to rally, but one drive ended when Bobby Dillon intercepted a Brown pass, and Larry Lauer later recovered a fumbled punt. The Packers had pulled off the upset, opening their new stadium by beating the only team that ever really mattered.

It was, of course, the perfect start to what would be a great season, except that it wasn't. The next week, in the second game at the new stadium, Green Bay lost to Detroit.

The Packers lost the only other game they played at the new stadium that year, too—to the New York Giants—and finished with another dismal record of 3-9. Blackbourn resigned after that season, and assistant coach Ray "Scooter" McLean took over. He lasted one season after the Packers limped in with a 1-10-1 record in 1958. That's when the Packers turned to the obscure line coach from the New York Giants.

It was 1965 when the Packers organization decided to rename the stadium in honor of the team founder and perhaps the most seminal figure in its development—Curly Lambeau. Since then, Lambeau Field has become one of the most recognized sports venues in the world.

But it wasn't a decision that thrilled everyone. Vince Lombardi, who had brought the Packers back from oblivion in 1959, couldn't understand why Lambeau got the honor when it was clear Lombardi had done much of the most recent work. Indeed, 1965 would mark the year the Packers won their first of three straight NFL titles, and those would be tacked on to the two Lombardi had already won.

But he didn't want to make a massive issue of the move and was placated when the Packers decided to rename Highland Avenue, which ran next to the stadium, "Lombardi Avenue."

WHAT BECAME OF RON KRAMER?

To this day, Ron Kramer has no regrets about the decision he made to leave the Packers after the 1964 season. In truth, there was really no decision to make.

"People got the impression that Vince got rid of me, and he didn't," Kramer said. "I told him, 'I don't want to leave you because you're the best coach I've ever been around.' I still love Green Bay, but family came first. Family is much more important."

Kramer was still at the height of his career in 1964. He had missed the 1958 season due to military obligations, but when he returned in 1959, he became an integral part of the Packers' building juggernaut. From 1961 to 1964, he caught 138 passes and scored 15 touchdowns and was named All-Pro in 1962 and 1963. He was also part of two NFL championship teams in 1961 and 1962.

He could see as well as anyone that the Packers were still a powerhouse in 1964 and he wanted to be a part of it. But circumstances changed dramatically prior to the 1965 season when Kramer's seven-year-old son Kurt lost an eye playing with a pair of scissors. The family was living in Detroit at the time and would not move to Green Bay under those circumstances, so Kramer did the only thing he felt he could do—he joined them. Kramer played out his option with the Packers and signed with the hometown Detroit Lions.

But he didn't leave without making sure the tight end position was in good hands.

"I told Vince that I would not leave Green Bay without teaching everything I know to [rookie] Marv Fleming," he said. "I said that Marv Fleming will know everything about playing tight end here."

Kramer played three years for the Lions with something less than terrific results. He caught 59 passes and scored one touchdown in that time, but while the Packers were winning three more championships, the Lions won a grand total of 15 games.

"I could have had five championships," he says now. "But I don't regret anything."

Kramer retired after the 1967 season and dabbled in many business ventures, some successful and some not. He was in the steel business for a while, and in 1981 he went bankrupt and lost $7 million. Then he went into the advertising and public relations business, where he's been ever since. He has been president of Ron Kramer Industries for the past 23 years, and his life continues to revolve around football in general and the Packers in particular.

He rarely misses a chance to meet up with his old friends and recall the good old days when they were all part of what was the best team in pro football. He may not raise hell like he did in his youth with his running buddy Hornung, but none of them ever miss a chance to remember what it used to be like.

"I'll never forget playing for the Packers," said Kramer, who also owns 130 acres of land south of Flint, Michigan. "Those were some of the best days of my life."

CHAPTER 11

SANTANA DOTSON

"It was like a lion walking through a slaughterhouse."

Name: Santana Dotson
Birthdate: December 19, 1969
Hometown: New Orleans, Louisiana
Current residence: Houston, Texas
Position: Defensive tackle
Height: 6-5
Playing weight: 285
Years: 1996-2001
College: Baylor University
Accomplishments: Signed as an unrestricted free agent with the Packers in 1996...Began his pro career with the Tampa Bay Buccaneers where he was NFL defensive rookie of the year in 1992...Played in 121 consecutive games from 1992-99.
The game: San Francisco 49ers, January 4, 1997 at Lambeau Field

THE LIFE OF SANTANA DOTSON

Named after the great Native American chief, the name Santana means "With unity there's strength" and it is a creed that has always been a part of the essential makeup of Santana Dotson.

He came from good stock; that was a given, since his dad was a former NFL lineman in his own right—Alphonse Dotson, who was a second-round draft pick of the Packers in 1965 out of Grambling but who chose to play for Kansas City of the rival AFL instead. So young Santana had the bloodlines, but he also knew there were no guarantees of anything in the game. And he found he had to prove himself everywhere he went.

He was born in New Orleans. The family moved to Houston when he was a kid, and he became a three-year star football player at Jack Yates High School. A prep All-American, he decided to attend Baylor University, where he continued his steady development. He was a three-year starter for the Bears as well as a three-time All-Southwest Conference pick. As a senior, he was an All-American, a finalist for both the Outland and Lombardi trophies, and the conference Defensive Player of the Year.

He finished his college career with 193 tackles and 18 sacks, and he was a fifth-round draft pick of the Tampa Bay Buccaneers in 1992.

As a rookie, he led the Bucs in quarterback sacks with 10, and he added 71 tackles and earned NFL Defensive Rookie of the Year honors. The sky, it appeared, was the limit for Dotson.

But as Dotson discovered, the things that are worth having are often the things that are the toughest to get and usually require the longest road to find.

He learned that more quickly than he ever figured he would in Tampa Bay. One year, he was the next great defensive lineman on a team still trying to find its foothold. The next year the rumors began, in back halls and in hushed tones at first, that Dotson didn't play hard every down. Then they grew a little louder, that he

Santana Dotson. *Harry How/Getty Images*

was lazy, that he had a bad attitude, that he thought he was better than the talent around him.

Rumors like that can be a disaster for any player, especially one still trying to prove himself. The rumors hurt and confused Dotson, because those were sins he had never, ever been accused of before. Not playing every down? Please. Lazy? Me? He was shocked and angry and, in a kind of self-fulfilling prophecy, his play did start to trail off and the Bucs continued to struggle.

After four years in Tampa, it seemed obvious he couldn't stay. The atmosphere was poisonous and he had worn out his welcome. Despite racking up 23 quarterback sacks and 195 tackles in four seasons, he jumped at an offer to sign with the Packers in 1996.

"I have to give credit to [Packers general manager] Ron Wolf," Dotson said. "I always had a belief in myself that I could do the job. What came from Tampa about me not playing every down and not holding up the whole season wasn't true. But as soon as I stepped in the building in Green Bay, they made it clear I was their guy. They said that if I went there, I was their guy and they felt I was the missing piece on the defense. I had a chance to stay in the same division [as Tampa Bay] and the biggest suitors were Minnesota and Green Bay. And when I watched the Packers lose the NFC championship the year before, I knew they could use my services. There was never any doubt from the Packers."

THE SETTING

The Packers had barely returned to their locker room in Texas Stadium after losing the 1995 NFC title game to the Dallas Cowboys when the talk already turned to the next season.

The Packers knew they were close. The loss to the Cowboys, in which Green Bay had dominated for three quarters before collapsing in the final 12 minutes, proved that they were on the verge of greatness. And on the plane ride home, coach Mike Holmgren pleaded with his guys not to forget how this loss felt and do something about it.

They did. With the addition of Dotson and safety Eugene Robinson, the defense was set. With a year's maturity in Brett Favre, the offense was in good hands. There was also the practically ignored signing of a former Heisman Trophy winner who was a too-small wide receiver who returned kicks. He was looking for a new opportunity in Green Bay—his name was Desmond Howard.

So the pieces were clearly in place, and when *Sports Illustrated* announced in August that the Packers would play the Chiefs in Super Bowl XXXI in New Orleans, the expectations tripled.

"It was hard to be picked right out of the blocks like that," Dotson said. "But I knew on paper the defense was going to be good. The only thing that was missing was the lack of a bad guy, a rebel, somebody who wasn't going to take anything from anybody."

But the Packers found some of those guys too. Dotson recalled a game in the Metrodome where the Vikings hit Favre out of bounds.

"We looked at each other and said, 'You know we have to answer that,'" Dotson said. "So on the next series [linebacker] Wayne Simmons took [Vikings running back] Amp Lee and just twirled him around. That's how we answered, and from there on we outhit everybody we played."

But there was still that hurdle to overcome. Despite a 13-3 record and domination of the NFC Central, the Packers really hadn't proven anything. They needed to reach the Super Bowl and win it. But first, the 49ers stood in their way.

THE GAME OF MY LIFE
By Santana Dotson

The biggest thing that sticks in my mind is leaving my situation in Tampa and going to Green Bay. Everybody will always talk about the offense [during the 1996 season] and how formidable they were. But the thing that sticks out in my mind was how strong the defense was. That sticks out to me as being a part of the best defensive line I've ever seen. Gilbert Brown, Reggie White,

Sean Jones, those were great players and we loved looking at the offensive linemen and seeing the looks on their faces every play as they tried to decide who they were going to double-team. It was almost like a lion walking through a slaughterhouse. You knew somebody was going to eat.

We were the kind of defense that year that we felt if somebody scored more than 17 points on us, it was a problem. We took a lot of pride in that. What a lot of people didn't know was that it was 22 guys who were in that room together and who enjoyed being around each other. If we were done with practice at three, we stuck around until four-thirty or five. We genuinely enjoyed the game and being around each other.

We knew that whole season that we could be something special, but we also knew we hadn't really proven anything until we beat the teams we had to beat in the playoffs and got to the Super Bowl. I remember that besides the Super Bowl that year, I didn't sleep the night before the game with San Fran. I recall so much of the hoopla from that game. We had beaten them earlier in the season at home, and it's very difficult to beat Super Bowl-caliber teams.

That morning I remember it was 35 degrees and rainy, and it was the coldest game I'd ever played at Lambeau. I remember I just couldn't get warm. But it was cold and so wet they turned off the seat warmers on the bench because they didn't want anybody to get shocked. And we thought, "Yeah, we're cold, but the other team is even colder," and we used to that to our advantage. I remember [49ers wide receiver] Jerry Rice went in at halftime and changed his whole uniform and he came out all nice and clean. We made a point on the first play of the second half to get him dirty again. And on that first play I looked up and there was [cornerback] Craig Newsome and [linebacker] Wayne Simmons knocking him to the ground just to make sure he was muddy again.

It was the mud bowl, and to me it was perfect Packers weather. You had the sushi eaters from California with their nice suits and they had to come to Lambeau Field. It was perfect weather for us because you had to peel yourself out of your uniform afterward.

In 1996, tackle Santana Dotson proved to be the final piece in the NFL's most dominant defense. *Brian Bahr/Getty Images*

We were a defense that took it one quarter at a time, and we talked about being dominant all the time. We'd say how we had to win one quarter and then this half and then this game and we're going to do the things we're supposed to do. We talked each week about every game being a stepping stone, and that 49ers game was a huge one.

GAME RESULT

If it had been five degrees colder, perhaps 15 inches of snow would have fallen on this miserable January day. Instead, a cold, miserable, unforgiving rain pounded down, soaking everything and everyone.

It was great.

The Packers had earned home field advantage and planned to take full advantage of it against a 49ers team that still harbored serious doubts about how good the Packers really were. Several 49ers had been quoted that week saying that the Packers had proven nothing to anyone until they won it all. And, in truth, the Packers couldn't argue the point.

But in front of a packed house at Lambeau Field, the Packers made believers even of the 49ers.

Desmond Howard brought a punt back 71 yards for the first touchdown, and the next time he touched the ball, he returned a punt 46 yards to the 49ers' seven-yard line, setting up a Favre-to-Andre Rison touchdown. An Edgar Bennett touchdown run made it 21-0 before San Francisco cut that lead to 21-7 by halftime.

After a mix-up on the opening kickoff of the second half that resulted in a fumble, the 49ers closed to 21-14 on an Elvis Grbac touchdown run. That's when the Packers found the extra gear that champions always discover.

Favre took the Packers on a 72-yard drive, throwing the ball only twice in a 12-play march, and the Packers scored a touchdown to recapture the momentum. Later in the fourth quarter, after a 49ers turnover, Bennett scored again and the Packers had the decisive 35-14 win.

Green Bay gained just 210 total yards in the slop, but that's all that was needed. Favre threw for just 79 yards, and the ground game came up big with 139 yards between Bennett and Dorsey Levens.

The next step had been accomplished.

WHAT BECAME
OF SANTANA DOTSON?

Over and above everything else, football is a business, and no one knew that better than Santana Dotson. The Packers had given him another chance after Tampa Bay. They had ignored the rumors and made their own decisions, and the result was that Dotson helped the Packers to two straight Super Bowls, two division titles and five trips to the playoffs. But times change, as they always must.

In 1999, he missed his first game ever with an injury, and in 2000 he suffered a torn quadriceps muscle. In 2001 a serious neck injury early in the season made him ineffective. The years were catching up to him.

Because of the injuries and the Packers' unwillingness to pay the unrestricted free agent what he wanted, the Packers released Dotson in July 2002. The consummate team player who had seen his career reborn in Green Bay was out of work, though not for long. He signed with the Washington Redskins, but in training camp he tore his Achilles' tendon.

"The first nine years of my career I didn't miss a game, and then all this started happening," he said. "But my grandmother put it best. She said, "The game has been good to you. You're 34 and your body's telling you something.""

So, reluctantly, Dotson retired.

"You want to do it forever, but you can't," he said. "I miss it, but I don't miss Monday mornings and the pain that came with it."

He remains among the Packers' all-time leaders in sacks with 26, and he finished with 248 tackles. But Dotson's contributions

GAME OF MY LIFE

went far beyond the statistics. He was the steadying force and the versatile athlete the Packers needed to solidify the defensive line.

"I just made a point to show my teammates what I could do," he said.

Dotson lives in Houston with his family and spends much of his time running his charitable Santana Dotson Foundation that also has a chapter in Milwaukee. He's trying to take time to expand the foundation regionally and, he hopes, nationally.

Dotson also stays busy in real estate ventures and coaching his nephew, Alonzo Dotson, who will play football this fall for Oklahoma.

"Things have been good," he said. "My son [Khari] is eight and my daughters are seven and three. My boy loves Lambeau Field and he misses it. I have season tickets to the Houston Texans, but he'd much rather sit on the couch and watch."

CHAPTER 12

JOHN BROCKINGTON

"I could do no wrong."

Name: John Stanley Brockington
Birthdate: September 7, 1948
Hometown: Brooklyn, New York
Current residence: San Diego, California
Position: Running back
Height: 6-1
Playing weight: 230
Years: 1971-77
College: Ohio State
Accomplishments: All-Pro in 1971 and 1973...First-team All-NFC in 1972...Named to Pro Bowl in 1971, 1972 and 1973...NFC Rookie of the Year in 1971...Inducted into Packers Hall of Fame in 1984.
The games: November 1, 1971 against the Detroit Lions at Milwaukee County Stadium; November 7, 1971 against the Chicago Bears at Soldier Field; November 14, 1971 against the Minnesota Vikings at Metropolitan Stadium.

THE LIFE OF JOHN BROCKINGTON

From New York City, John Brockington was something to see for the fans of Ohio State football. He had the size of a full-back but the moves and speed and agility of a halfback. He was one of those classic players who would just as soon gain yardage by running over you than running around you. And he found himself part of some of the best college football teams in history.

"[Ohio State coach] Woody Hayes was so positive," Brockington said. "He'd say, 'This is how you'll execute,' and we did. In three years on the varsity, we never went into a game thinking somebody was better than we were. We never went into a game thinking we were going to lose. That's a hell of a mindset."

And in three seasons, from 1968-70, few were better than the Buckeyes. Ohio State won the national title in 1968, finished fourth nationally in 1969 with an 8-1 record and won a disputed national title in 1970 after going through the regular season 9-0 before losing to Stanford in the Rose Bowl. Brockington pounded his way to 1,142 yards and 17 touchdowns that season and was named one of four Ohio State All-Americans.

The senior class of 1970, which featured Brockington, line-backer Jim Stillwagon and defensive back Mike Sensibaugh, finished their three-year varsity careers with a 27-2 record, three Big Ten titles and two national championships.

In the 1971 NFL draft, the Packers had the ninth pick over-all and knew they needed to overhaul their rushing attack that was beginning to break down. With first-year coach Dan Devine, who favored the more conservative running attack anyway, Brockington was the ideal choice.

THE SETTING

It was a shock in more ways than one for Brockington as he went from the supremely confident, almost arrogant, world of Ohio State to the NFL. In Columbus, Brockington had been told, and

John Brockington. *Vernon J. Biever photo*

had come to believe it with his entire being, that no one was better. But in Green Bay, the mood shifted dramatically.

"I get to the pros and Dan says, 'They're quicker than you are and they're faster than you are,'" he said. "He was the most mealy-mouthed coach I'd ever had. He was always criticizing things."

Packers fans found it hard to believe that they were just four years removed from the iconic and mourned Vince Lombardi, who could make his players fly through a wall and smile while doing it.

But Devine was a far different animal. Quiet and oh-so-conservative, Devine replaced Phil Bengston, a Lombardi lieutenant, after Bengston decided three years was enough trying to outrun a shadow.

Bengston's three years had produced just one winning season, and Devine was brought in from the University of Missouri to instill a new attitude that had no particular ties to the Green Bay Packers of the previous decade.

He brought in a run-the-ball-first mentality and emphasized defense. He slowly started to phase out all the Packers from the previous era, including quarterback Bart Starr, in favor of the young, smart Scott Hunter. He also slipped youngster Jim Carter in at middle linebacker to replace legendary Ray Nitschke, and Brockington stepped in as the featured runner.

A new era had begun, whether anyone wanted it to or not.

THE GAME OF MY LIFE
By John Brockington

My game was really three games. Monday night in Milwaukee against the Lions and against the Bears and Vikings. Those games are what put me on the path to my first 1,000-yard year. They really didn't run me that much in 1971 [216 carries in 14 games], but I remember I really got into a groove. I had my first 100-yard game against the Bengals [on October 3], and that's when I said, "OK, now I'm getting warmed up."

But then came the Detroit game on Monday night in the rain. It was awful. It was rainy and nasty. It was so wet and slushy I wondered what kind of game we'd have. The first play was a draw play and there was such a big hole that I thought, "Man, I could've gotten a big one," but I was tripped up in the hole.

But we ran 37 Slant, off tackle to the right, all night. That was the bread and butter play for my career. It seemed every time I got the ball, there was a hole. I had a really big night for the amount of carries I had.

The Bears game was next. I remember the night before the game [quarterback] Scott Hunter, [cornerback] Charlie Hall and I went out to dinner in downtown Chicago. It was this overblown Chicago restaurant and there was a beefeater at the door and he'd always say, "Welcome, senator." He called everybody "senator." This restaurant had a great bar and this two-pound steak, and after we were done I thought we wouldn't be worth a damn the next day.

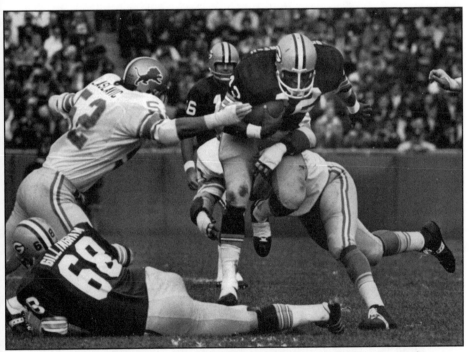

John Brockington's three-game outburst against Detroit, Chicago and Minnesota established him as one of the NFL's top young running backs. *Vernon J. Biever photo*

But it was a big rival for us, and I had a great game. Everything I touched, it worked. I was running through some serious holes. One play, it was like third down and 19 and we called a draw play. I went through the hole, cut to the right and got like 20 yards. On the closing drive [to win the game] it was pitch right, pitch left and I was getting yards. I said, "This is easy."

Then came the Vikings game. The first time we played them that season [a 24-13 loss in Green Bay] I couldn't get to the hole. The Vikings defense was super fast. But by the second game, I was more mature and things started slowing down in my mind. I'd get 10 yards, five yards a carry. It was like I was greased.

Those games were so significant to me because they put me on the track for 1,000 yards. I was in a serious zone for those three games. I could do no wrong. That's when the season really got fun.

I remember once listening to this speech from the National University Center for Peak Performance and they talked about all these athletes and when they're trying to get to their peak performance. They talked about being in a zone and it's an amazing thing. Everything slows down. You're running and you can do no wrong. I can see things. I can cut back. When you're like that you just want the ball. But I never had a string of games like that again.

GAME RESULTS

When John Brockington entered his three-game "zone," the Packers were effectively going nowhere in a hurry. Through six games, Green Bay was sputtering along with a 2-4 record that had included wins over two of the AFC's weakest entrants— Denver and Cincinnati—and an ignominious 42-40 opening-day loss to the Giants in which Devine had his leg broke after a sideline collision.

Into County Stadium came the Detroit Lions for a Monday night game that had to be played in a constant, dreary downpour. But a national audience got to see the new, young back out of Ohio State who was going to make the Packers relevant again.

Knowing the weather wasn't going to cooperate, Devine was at his conservative best, allowing Hunter to throw just five passes all night. The bulk of the offense would fall to Brockington, and he came through superbly.

He rushed only 16 times, but he gained 111 yards in a game that ended up 14-14. In fact, it was 14-14 at halftime thanks to a last-second 49-yard Greg Landry-to-Charley Sanders touchdown pass. The Packers' two scores came on short runs by Dave Hampton and Hunter.

Green Bay had opportunities in the second half, but 36-year-old field goal kicker Lou Michaels missed from 39 and 44 yards in the muck. In the end, the Packers gained just 218 total yards, all on the ground, while the Lions managed just 290 yards. But for the Packers, at least, a tie wasn't a loss. And the Lions came away impressed with Brockington.

"I'll tell you," All-Pro linebacker Mike Lucci said afterward. "The Packers didn't waste their first draft pick."

The following Sunday at Soldier Field, Brockington was even better. He plowed over the Bears for 142 yards on 30 carries and scored on a seven-yard run. His 30 carries were just two shy of the club record set in 1967 by Jim Grabowski.

Green Bay led the game 14-0 at halftime before the Bears tied it late in the fourth quarter. But on the kickoff, Hampton, who had already fumbled four times in the game, brought the kick back 62 yards to the Bears' 39. That's when Brockington took over, carrying six straight times down to the Chicago 15. Michaels then connected on a 22-yard field goal with 59 seconds left to win the game, 17-14.

The last game in his remarkable journey came in Minneapolis against the powerful Vikings. And while the Packers dominated nearly every aspect of the game, they also made a ton of mistakes and ended up losing 3-0.

Brockington pounded out 149 yards on 23 carries, which may have been the best accomplishment of the three 100-yard games, since the Vikings had easily the toughest defense in the NFC. The Packers ended up with 245 rushing yards, an unheard-of total against the Vikings. The defense also held the Vikings to five first downs and 87 total yards.

Unfortunately for the Packers, they also committed four turnovers, including a Donny Anderson fumble deep in Minnesota territory, two missed field goals by Michaels and failing on two shots from the Vikings' one.

The decisive play came with eight minutes left when, again deep in Minnesota territory, Hunter decided against the safe run and tried to hit tight end Rich McGeorge for a touchdown. The ball was intercepted by Charlie West and brought back to mid-field. Eventually Fred Cox kicked a 25-yard field goal that ended up being the final score.

It was a frustrated and angry Packers locker room afterward, and Brockington said it best: "God must not dig somebody on this team."

Brockington's three-game total was 402 yards and he finished the season with 1,105 yards, earning him NFC Rookie of the Year honors. But the Packers' fortunes weren't any brighter as they finished 4-8-2, their worst mark since 1958.

WHAT BECAME OF JOHN BROCKINGTON?

There was no reason to believe 1972 would be any better, but in the bizarre world of the NFL, nothing is ever as it seems. The Packers caught lightning in a bottle, got steady play from Hunter, superb seasons from rookies Willie Buchanon and Chester Marcol and used the tandem of Brockington and MacArthur Lane in the backfield to dominate teams.

With Brockington rushing for 1,027 yards and Lane adding another 821 yards, the Packers won the NFC Central Division with a 10-4 record. In the playoffs, though, the Washington Redskins employed a five-man front to shut down the Packers' running game and made them throw. The Packers never did. Brockington was held to nine yards on 13 carries, and Washington prevailed 16-3. That result still rankles Brockington.

"We'd run into that five-man front two weeks earlier and [offensive coordinator] Bart Starr said if they do that again, run two backs out of the backfield and throw it. But Dan never did it because he decided he wanted to coach that day. Nobody could believe we let that happen. I ran into [Redskins linebacker] Chris Hanburger a few weeks later and he said, 'Why didn't you guys throw the ball? We didn't expect to stay in that defense all day.'"

Brockington didn't know it at the time, but that would be his first and last taste of the playoffs. He ran for another 1,144 yards in 1973, but the Packers fell back to 5-7-2. In 1974, he managed just 883 yards and Green Bay was just 6-8, and that cost Devine his job.

Starr took over and made changes of his own, including trading Lane to Kansas City and reducing Brockington's role in the offense. The former 1,000-yard rusher squeezed out just 434 yards in 1975, and Green Bay sank to 4-10. Brockington was clashing with new offensive coordinator Paul Roach, and he decided a change of scenery was needed. He asked for a trade in 1977 and the Packers complied, dealing him to Kansas City.

He finished out the 1977 season with the Chiefs, gaining 161 yards and finishing his pro career with 5,185 yards and 30 touchdowns. By 1978, he was out of football.

Immediately after leaving football, he got into the financial services business in San Diego and he's been there ever since.

CHAPTER 13

JAMES LOFTON

"We felt we had something good."

Name: James David Lofton
Birthdate: July 5, 1956
Hometown: Los Angeles, California
Current residence: San Diego, California
Position: Wide receiver
Height: 6-3
Playing weight: 192
Years: 1978-86
College: Stanford
Accomplishments: Inducted into Pro Football Hall of Fame in 2003...Named to eight Pro Bowls, seven with the Packers and including six in a row in Green Bay from 1980-85...Named All-Pro four times...Named All-NFC three times...Inducted into Packers Hall of Fame in 1999.
The game: New York Giants, September 20, 1982 at The Meadowlands

THE LIFE OF JAMES LOFTON

It almost seems James Lofton was born to be an NFL wide receiver the way William Shakespeare was born to be a writer. Blessed with ideal size, great speed and the kind of languid athleticism that made it look like he was hardly even trying sometimes, Lofton set the standard for what would become the prototypical pro wide receiver that we see today. But in the 1970s, he was considered something extraordinary.

Born in Fort Ord, California, he was a standout athlete at Los Angeles's Washington High School. He took that ability to Stanford University and blossomed into one of the nation's best college receivers. While at Stanford, he caught 68 passes for 1,216 yards and he set a single-season NCAA record in 1977 with 12 touchdown receptions. But he was more than a football star as he earned All-America honors four straight years in the long jump. Perhaps most important of all, Lofton earned his bachelor's degree in industrial engineering.

But as well rounded as Lofton already was coming out of college, everyone knew his future was in football. Certainly the Green Bay Packers knew it, and they made him their first of two first-round draft picks in 1978, the sixth pick overall. And immediately he made that pick pay off.

In 1977, the Packers' top receiver was fullback Barty Smith, who caught just 37 passes. With Lofton, the Packers could actually become a wide receiver-oriented offense again and caught 46 passes, averaged nearly 18 yards a catch and caught six of the 11 touchdown passes Packers quarterbacks managed to throw that season. That would be his last season (except for the strike-shortened 1982 season) that Lofton would catch fewer than 50 passes for the Packers.

In 1983 and 1984, he led the NFL in receptions with 58 and 62 catches, respectively, and he became perhaps the NFL's most dangerous deep threat.

James Lofton. *Vernon J. Biever photo*

THE SETTING

The NFL owners and the players, quite simply, were in the midst of a civil war as the 1982 season began.

The threat of a strike had loomed for a while, but as with most unsavory topics, nobody really wanted to deal with the reality of the situation until it was too late. The issues were as simple, and as complicated, as free agency and salaries. The NFL had fought the concept of one player leaving his team to join another for a long time. But times were changing, and NFL players had seen how successful baseball players had been in their quest for free agency.

So the topic finally bubbled to the surface in 1982, and when the current NFL Players Association contract ran out and no agreement was reached, a strike date was set. Players knew what the future held, and it wasn't pretty.

Remember, this wasn't the NFL of today, the NFL that was made possible in a large part by the walkout that occurred in 1982. Players then did not make millions of dollars in signing bonuses that could be deferred, if necessary, forever. This was a strictly salary business, and if you didn't play, you didn't get paid.

But the cause was important enough that most of the players were solid behind the union and walked out willingly when the time came. And this was an especially contentious strike, with charges and countercharges being leveled by both management and players alike.

For the Packers, this was a critical time. The pieces seemed to be in place for this team to do some damage in the NFC Central Division. The offense had found its stride and was as dangerous as any in football. The defense could do the job, but it was going to be the offense that led this team.

Lofton knew, like players on so many other teams knew, that solidarity was key to being successful once the strike ended. Players needed to hang together, stay in town, practice together and support each other, because if they didn't, the results could be disastrous.

Once the strike was called, the Packers did indeed stay together.

"I remember we got back on our charter plane and got back to Green Bay in the wee hours of the morning," Lofton said. "We met the next day in a local park and we talked as a team. I remembered we practiced at a high school in DePere and the media came out a little at the beginning. Mike Douglass and I officiated Pop Warner football games and other guys were trying to do a lot of things just to stay active."

But no one knew how long the strike would last, and with no paychecks coming in, it was a tough time, especially for younger players who had almost nothing.

"I'm sure there were some landlords who were lenient with the rents," Lofton said.

Finally, after 57 days, an agreement was reached. The last game had been played September 21 and the walkout lasted until November 16. In the interim, seven games had been lost and could not be made up. As it was, the Super Bowl had to be pushed back to January 30 and the divisions had to be scrapped in favor of a "tournament" in which eight teams from each conference would earn playoff berths.

The Packers finished third with a solid 5-3-1 record and hosted the No. 6 St. Louis Cardinals. In Green Bay's first playoff game since 1972 and its first at home since 1967, the Packers blasted St. Louis 41-6 before going to Dallas and losing to the Cowboys, 37-26. Green Bay's next playoff game would not come for another 10 years.

THE GAME OF MY LIFE
By James Lofton

The reasons I believe this game was significant are twofold — No. 1, I was on the executive committee of the NFL Players Association and I knew that following the game we'd go on strike.

We'd started off with a win the very first week of the regular season, and I knew that since we were going to go on strike, one of the most important things to keep our team together was to win this game. If you don't win then everybody drops their heads for a couple of days and they take off for different parts of the country. We were able to win, and qualifying for the playoffs was important.

We had beaten the Rams in a comeback win in Milwaukee and then we turned around and beat the Giants 27-19. I had a couple of big plays—a reverse and a long catch. But it was a game we felt like we could give away. It was Monday night. It was the national stage. With so much fooling around between the players and owners, the game took on a bigger magnitude.

We had had so many meetings leading up to the strike, and I tried to keep the guys abreast of the negotiations and the offers. It was a real taxing time for me personally. When you're trying to get 50 guys in a consensus, it's tough. They had a strike fund set up, but in 1982, the average salary was $50,000, so most guys would come back after the strike without money.

I remember we were pretty well united as a team. The guys were behind me. I had great support. At the time we were trying to get a system in place, we were trying to get free agency, a wage scale. But the owners were saying we're never going to allow you to get free agency, we'll never let you be free.

So the game was in New York, and it was the final game before the strike deadline. I think the strike actually started while the game was still being played, because it was a midnight deadline. The other significant thing about the game was that the lights went out twice. You think about the unions who were supporting the players, and you always wonder if they had something to do with it. But there were 68,000 fans there, and I don't recall them being adversarial toward us.

I really think that if we had lost that game the guys would have splintered, so we talked about it before the game and said how we needed to win. We felt we had something good. I think if we had 16 games that season we would have 11. That's how good we thought we were.

James Lofton (80) was an integral part of one of the most powerful and innovative offenses the NFL had ever seen. *Vernon J. Biever photo*

I remember once the strike ended, it was the best feeling to be back on the field. And we hadn't even played in Green Bay yet. We started the season in Milwaukee and then went to New York and our next game [after the strike ended] was in Milwaukee against the Vikings. Then we went to New York to play the Jets. Playing was a gift we were allowed to have for a short period, and then to have it taken away from us for almost half the season. But we stayed together.

GAME RESULT

Both the New York Giants and Green Bay Packers understood the significance of what was about to occur that night. It was the last game before a strike—potentially debilitating—was about to be called. It could last a week, it could last a month, or it could last the entire season. No one really knew.

But this much every player did know—they had to show solidarity to the cause, and while 62,000 or so fans hooted from the stands, players from both teams went to midfield prior to the game and shook hands in a show of strength that the owners surely didn't want to see.

The game itself was important, as Lofton said. But in other ways, it was just an afterthought, an event that had to be completed only because it was on the schedule. More than a few players were already thinking about the next day, and the day after that. Still, if it was going to be played, it might as well be played the best way possible.

The Giants took command early and led 19-7 late in the third quarter when Lofton made the play that turned the game around. With 1:37 left in the third quarter, Lofton took an end-around hand off from Lynn Dickey and went practically untouched for an 83-yard touchdown. That changed the momentum completely.

In the fourth quarter, Eddie Lee Ivery ran for an 11-yard touchdown and Jan Stenerud kicked field goals of 37 and 22 yards as Green Bay rolled to the 27-19 win.

Dickey completed 13 of 20 passes for 203 yards, and Lofton finished with four receptions for 101 yards. Overall the Packers outgained New York 363 total yards to 267. But for many the result was lost in the fact that the next day they would be on strike. And while they didn't know it then, the strike would last nearly two months.

WHAT BECAME OF JAMES LOFTON?

The mid-1980s proved to be turbulent years both on and off the field for the Packers. As their fortunes continued to flounder in the standings, a series of brutal public relations disasters off the field continued to sully the reputation of one of pro sports' most storied franchises.

In 1986, coach Forrest Gregg, now in his third season, decided to cut loose some popular veteran players like tight end Paul Coffman, defensive end Mike Butler and linebacker Mike Douglass. Defensive end Charles Martin was suspended by the NFL for two games for his body slam and subsequent injury of Bears quarterback Jim McMahon. To come later was the holdout of quarterback Randy Wright and first-round draft pick Brent Fullwood, continued problems with Martin and the conviction of cornerback Mossy Cade for second-degree sexual assault.

Caught up in the web, to the shock of nearly everyone, was James Lofton. He was a model citizen, a terrific player, a record-setting wide receiver and one of the few bright spots for a franchise desperate for anything to go right.

But late in the 1986 season he was charged with second-degree sexual assault for an incident in a Milwaukee hotel, forcing the Packers to keep Lofton from playing in the season finale in New York against the Giants—a game the Packers tanked 55-24.

Though he was cleared of all charges, the Packers decided it was best to cut ties with the receiver. So despite catching what was then a club-record 530 passes for 9,656 yards (still a team record) and 49 touchdowns, in April 1987 Green Bay traded him to the Los Angeles Raiders for a third- and fourth-round draft pick.

Lofton proved that, even after nine seasons in Green Bay, he still had plenty left in the gas tank. After two seasons in Los Angeles, he signed with the Buffalo Bills in 1989 and was part of three AFC championship teams and three Super Bowl appearances. He closed out his career with short stints with the Rams and Eagles before retiring in 1993.

He became the first player to surpass 14,000 yards in receptions, and he was the first NFL player to score touchdowns in three decades. He finished with 764 receptions (10th all-time) and 75 touchdowns.

After retirement Lofton joined CNN as a pro football analyst from 1994-96, then went to NBC in 1997, returned to CNN in 1998 and then was a game analyst for Fox from 1998-2001. He also handled the preseason color commentary for the Carolina Panthers from 1995-2001.

But despite all that TV work, Lofton could never shake the feeling that he wanted, and needed, to coach.

"I had always known that but I was just delaying it to spend more time with my family," he said. "I was coaching my kids a little bit, and I wanted to have an impact on their lives."

Indeed, football has been passed down to his kids, as his son David is a quarterback at Stanford, and Daniel is a highly regarded high school receiver. Youngest daughter Rachel is a quality middle school athlete.

Lofton was lured back to coaching and will begin his third season as wide receivers coach for the San Diego Chargers. And after 18 years of playing, Lofton believes he has a unique ability to get the best out of today's young receivers.

"You're compiling the information you got as a player and as a broadcaster," he said. "I think I've got a good handle on what players are thinking."

Lofton's future goals consist of becoming a head coach, either at the pro or college level.

"We'll see," he said.

CHAPTER 14

DAVE ROBINSON

"As well as I played, I didn't get the game ball."

Name: David Richard Robinson
Birthdate: May 3, 1941
Hometown: Mount Laurel, New Jersey
Current residence: Akron, Ohio
Position: Linebacker
Height: 6-3
Playing weight: 240
Years: 1963-72
College: Penn State
Accomplishments: Named to Pro Bowl 1966, 1967 and 1969...Named All-Pro 1967, 1968 and 1969...Inducted into Packer Hall of Fame in 1982.
The game: Baltimore Colts, December 12, 1965 at Memorial Stadium

THE LIFE OF DAVE ROBINSON

Like so many players at the time, Dave Robinson was more than just a football player. He was another of the long line of athletes who could excel in anything they did. And, oh yeah, he was another in a long line of serious mama's boys.

Growing up without a father, he adored his mother, Mary, and like so many other moms, she didn't like her child playing football. But he was exceptional at it and earned a scholarship to Penn State, where he was not only an All-America defensive end but an All-America offensive end as well. But as he was thriving on the football field, he was also a star basketball player who managed to find time to earn his degree in engineering.

The Packers made him their first-round draft pick in 1963 with plans to move him from defensive end to linebacker. After studying for a year behind Dan Currie at left linebacker, Robinson stepped in as a starter in 1964 and never relinquished the role.

Dave Robinson. *Vernon J. Biever photo*

He became known for his uncanny ability to make the right play at the right time. When the Packers needed something big to happen on defense, he was there to make the play. He would come up with the interception or the fumble recovery or the quarterback pressure just when the Packers needed it most. And that often meant in games against the Colts, who were one of the Packers' great rivals in those days.

THE SETTING

Indeed, as the Dallas Cowboys were the great rivals a few years later, the Colts and Packers waged their share of epic battles earlier in the 1960s. These were two proud franchises that never gave an inch to each other because they didn't have to. But 1965 was clearly a year of war.

The Packers had already beaten the Colts once that season, a 20-17 victory in Milwaukee. They played again in Baltimore later that year with the Packers again winning 42-27. But that wouldn't be the end of it.

On December 26, the two teams met again for the Western Conference championship in Green Bay, and it was a game that would change the very way football was played and a game still talked about today.

"The reporters were asking us how difficult it was going to be to beat the Colts three times in one year," Robinson said. "Lombardi said, 'If you're better than they are, you can beat them 10 times in one year.' We thought, 'He's right. Let's beat them and get out of here.'"

And it figured to be easy, especially since Baltimore would have to play without both starting quarterback Johnny Unitas and backup Gary Cuozzo, both of whom were out with injuries. That forced the Colts to use halfback Tom Matte, who hadn't played quarterback since high school. With plays taped to his wrist, Matte did little more than hand the ball off or run it himself.

"We went into the game so confident," Robinson said. "Then when Bart Starr went out and we went, 'Uh-oh.'"

Sure enough, Starr left the game after only 21 seconds with a rib injury, forcing backup Zeke Bratkowski into the game. Now in a battle of survival, the Colts, with Matte frantically running the show, led 10-0 at halftime before Green Bay finally scored on a Paul Hornung run. That set up the play Colts players and fans still squawk about.

With time running out in regulation, Don Chandler kicked a 22-yard field goal that many, including Chandler, thought was wide right. But the kick was high above the upright, and the officials on the end line couldn't tell definitively if the kick was wide or right over the uprights. They called the kick good, and the Colts howled. To this day, Robinson insists the kick was good.

"I was on the field goal team and my eyes were a lot better then than they are now," he said. "Chandler knew he hit it bad and the kick kind of hung. But it was good. Back then the NFL had a rule that they wouldn't allow a TV camera behind the goal post, so you only had a two-dimensional view. You couldn't tell. But I knew."

In overtime, Chandler left no doubt, drilling a 25-yarder to win the game. The controversy swirled, though, and the next season, the uprights were lengthened so such indecision might be avoided in the future.

In 1966, the Colts had another chance to take out the Packers late in the season as Unitas drove them to what figured to be a late, game-winning touchdown. But Robinson hit Unitas and forced a fumble, and the Packers held on for the 14-10 win in Baltimore.

THE GAME OF MY LIFE
By Dave Robinson

It's a funny thing because all those games were big to me. But the biggest game to me was the 1965 game in Baltimore in the fog. That means a lot to me, and I still think about it a lot and what happened in that game.

I remember my mother was going to take a bus down to Baltimore [from the Philadelphia suburb of Mount Laurel, N.J.]

and she said she needed 42 tickets for the game. I really had to scurry around to find 42 tickets. Then she called that weekend and said she's sold all her tickets and didn't have any for herself or my two brothers. So I called my friend [and Colts tight end] John Mackey and he got more tickets for my brothers and my mother. She sat right in the middle of the most die-hard Colts fans, along with my brothers Leslie and Byron.

They said that the Colts fans were boisterous, but fun, people. I remember just before halftime we were up 13-3 or something like that and Jim Taylor fumbled on the [Packers'] six-yard line. My brother Byron said, "Don't worry, my brother's going to stop them," and he bet $50 on it. The next play [Colts quarterback] Gary Cuozzo tried to lob it into the end zone and I intercepted it and ran it back 80 yards to the Colts 10. Then Bart Starr threw a little pass to Boyd Dowler to score.

The guy paid off the bet, but that guy—I never did find out his name—insisted that my brother sit in the same seat every time we came to Baltimore to play.

That was a big game for me, because my family was there. That interception was the longest ever against the Baltimore Colts at the time, but I didn't score. Lenny Moore caught me. I remember on that play that the fullback flared out and he was my man. Cuozzo tried to lob it to him, and I just cut in front and intercepted it. I took it down the sideline and I slowed up to let somebody block Cuozzo. I got razzed [for not scoring] immediately if not sooner after I got to the bench. There was always somebody giving me a hard time.

But I had a good game. That same game, Paul Hornung scored five touchdowns, so as well as I played, I didn't even get the game ball.

GAME RESULT

While Paul Hornung will be remembered for his five touchdowns, it was that Robinson interception that turned the course of the game.

It was a horrendously foggy day in Baltimore, so bad in fact that many fans and the viewers on national TV simply couldn't see what was going on down on the field.

But the players knew only too well.

The Packers led the Colts 14-13 when Taylor fumbled the ball deep in Packers territory. A Baltimore score could be disastrous for the Packers, allowing the Colts to take a halftime lead and steal away the momentum.

On second down and two from the Packers' two, Cuozzo tried to hit fullback Jerry Hill out of the backfield, and that's when Robinson made his interception and returned the ball 87 yards to the Colts' 10. Two plays later Starr hit Boyd Dowler for the touchdown and a critical 21-13 lead.

"That was the big play," Lombardi said afterward. "They didn't score and we did. It changed the game."

Of course, Hornung had his say, too, scoring on three runs and two long passes from Starr. The defense held the Colts to 231 total yards while forcing three interceptions and two fumbles.

WHAT BECAME OF DAVE ROBINSON?

Dave Robinson always figured he'd retire as a Green Bay Packer.

"I didn't want to be one of those guys who had four or five teams behind his name," he said. "I wanted to retire as a Green Bay Packer."

But sometimes plans don't work out like you want them to. In 10 years with the Packers, Robinson redefined the outside linebacker position. He intercepted 21 passes and recovered nine fumbles and was the kind of athletic force that turned the position into what it is today.

After moving in as the starting left linebacker in 1964, Robinson didn't budge from that spot until 1970 when he missed 10 games with a ruptured Achilles tendon. He recovered and took back his spot in 1971 and 1972. But after the '72 season, coach Dan Devine wanted a younger and faster player in that position, and Robinson, despite his wishes to stay a Packer forever, was dealt to Washington for a second-round draft pick.

He seriously contemplated retirement, but Redskins coach George Allen, who was looking for veteran players to help revitalize the franchise, convinced him to play and he had two more solid seasons.

Robinson retired after the 1974 season and went to work for Schlitz Brewing in Akron.

"Schlitz was going to be a three-year assignment, and we've been here ever since," he said.

He said his years as a Packer helped him get into the business, of which he knew very little when he got started.

"The only thing I had was the Super Bowl rings," he said. "Because I was a member of the Packers, it allowed me to get in and see people. But if you didn't know what you were doing, you were out the door. Some people thought I was just a jock who didn't know a damn thing about business. I had to prove myself. I had to sell people on the fact that I knew what I was talking about."

Robinson did just that.

He formed Mars Distributing in 1984, but he has since sold the stock in the company. Now he calls himself "semiretired" and has a hand in selling field turf for a Montreal-based company. One of his assignments is trying to sell the turf to Milwaukee city high schools.

"It's always good to come back to Wisconsin," he said.

CHAPTER 15

PAUL COFFMAN

"We pulled out all the stops."

Name: Paul Randolph Coffman
Birthdate: March 29, 1956
Hometown: St. Louis, Missouri
Current residence: Peculiar, Missouri
Position: Tight end
Height: 6-3
Playing weight: 225
Years: 1978-85
College: Kansas State
Accomplishments: All-Pro 1984...First-team All-NFC in 1983 and 1984...Named to Pro Bowl 1982-84...Inducted into Packers Hall of Fame in 1994.
The game: Washington Redskins, October 17, 1983 at Lambeau Field

THE LIFE OF PAUL COFFMAN

He was a big farm kid from Kansas who wanted nothing more than a chance to prove himself.

At Kansas State, Coffman, with the endearing nickname "Hog," majored in grain milling and figured his future might lie somewhere on the farm. But he just wanted a chance. One chance.

So when Kansas State teammate and friend Gary Spani, a linebacker, was set to try out for Green Bay Packers assistant coach John Meyer, Coffman tagged along and asked Meyer to take a look at him, too.

Meyer was impressed with Coffman's athleticism and determination and the fact that he caught everything in sight. But he still went undrafted in 1978. A little while later, when the Packers needed a tight end to fill out the roster, Meyer remembered Coffman and the Packers signed him as a free agent. It was one of the great free agency decisions in team history.

He didn't catch a pass that season, but in 1979 he took over the spot from Rich McGeorge and became one of the game's most prolific pass-catching tight ends.

THE SETTING

By 1983, Bart Starr had used up nearly all of the good will and fond memories that he had built up in his 16 years as Packers quarterback. The fans remembered the good old days when he threw his strikes to Boyd Dowler and Max McGee, but good old days is just what they were—old. And with each passing year, the memories grew fainter and the frustration grew deeper.

Starr had taken over as head coach in 1975 from Dan Devine, and in the eight years that followed, he had taken the Packers to just one playoff berth and two winning records. It seemed with every step forward there were three steps back, and patience was running out on everybody's part. Were it any other coach besides the sainted Starr, he wouldn't have lasted four seasons. But Starr

Paul Coffman (82). *Vernon J. Biever photo*

was given an extra long leash with the hope that one day it would pay off.

The signs were there in 1982 when, despite a strike that cancelled half the season, the Packers cobbled together a 5-3-1 record, earned a playoff berth for the first time in 10 years and actually won in the postseason for the first time since the Ice Bowl.

All the pieces were in place for the Packers to make their return to the NFL's elite, and it would be even more perfect with Starr in charge.

But it never happened. The season started badly and only got worse. The Packers couldn't sign left end Mike Butler, and starting safety Maurice Harvey was waived. The Packers lost linebacker Randy Scott and nose tackle Rich Turner to season-ending injuries.

It was no coincidence that the damage all came to the defensive side of the ball and the Packers simply didn't have enough fingers for all the leaks sprouting in the dam. For most of the season, the Packers had to play defense with guys who didn't belong in the NFL. Sure there were the warriors like linebackers Mike Douglass and John Anderson and safety Johnnie Gray, but it simply wasn't enough, and these Packers set a record for futility on defense that went unmatched for years.

One of the highlights was certainly the Washington game, but the next week the Packers lost to Minnesota in overtime and then went to Cincinnati and got clobbered by the Bengals.

Despite the fact that Green Bay couldn't win stop anybody on defense, they still amazingly had a shot at the playoffs in the final week. But leading the Bears in the final minute, Starr refused to call his available timeouts and Chicago marched to the Packers' five, where Bob Thomas kicked a 22-yard field goal. Gray fumbled the kickoff and the season was done.

The next day Starr was fired, and Forrest Gregg, another voice from the golden past, took over.

THE GAME OF MY LIFE
By Paul Coffman

It seemed like in that era we were an average team, but we always thought we were better than that. We thought we should have won some of the games we were losing, but we could never get over that 8-8 situation we put ourselves in.

But this was one of the elite teams in the NFL coming into Lambeau Field on Monday night. What more could you ask for when you're an average team trying to prove yourself? It was exciting.

That week we saw something on film we thought we could take advantage of. [Offensive coordinator] Bob Schnelker was so detailed that he made sure you knew everything. He was that detailed. We knew we needed to hit on all cylinders and we knew we couldn't even punt if we wanted to win. We had to play lights-out.

And we had the athletes to do it. We had an offensive line that, because we didn't win much, they didn't get the recognition they deserved. But they really protected Lynn. We scored quite a few points that season, but we never had the killer defense that stuffed people. At times that came back to hurt us because Lynn would sometimes take chances he shouldn't have taken. He'd get a bad rap for throwing an interception when he should've taken a sack. But we had to take the chance because our defense wasn't going to stop anybody. They practiced hard, they did what they were supposed to do, but we just didn't have the horses to stop people. They just weren't big enough, strong enough, fast enough to make it happen.

But just the fact that it was the Super Bowl champions and Monday night football, that was enough. That scenario on Monday night football was exciting. I'd been to the Pro Bowl and watched Monday night games and I knew everybody would be watching, and I wanted to have a good game.

In pregame warmups people were already in their seats. It seemed from the get-go that the stadium was packed. People were hanging out of the stadium and we pulled out all the stops. We even had a play where we actually threw the ball back to Lynn. We had a short-yardage play where we handed it to Eddie Lee Ivery and he threw it back to me. We tried some things and they worked, and the Redskins had a pretty darned good defense.

I remember one play. Bob Schnelker was on the sidelines and he said, "Give me a fullback, give me a fullback" and a guy named Mike Meade stepped up. He gave Meade the play and sent him in. It's a play that would go to him if it worked out, and Schnelker realized it and said, "No, no, no." Lynn threw it to him in the flat, Meade ran for a touchdown, and Schnelker went from "No, no, no" to "Go, go, go." Everybody got into the act that night.

Down the stretch Gerry Ellis was going on an out route. Lynn hit him in the middle of the field, and there was no one around. It was like the seas parted. [Washington cornerback] Darrell Green finally caught him at the five. But the thing is, if he'd scored, it probably would have left another 45 seconds on the clock and Washington could have probably scored again. If that happened we wouldn't be talking about this now.

After the game, it was late and people have to go to work, but the whole stadium was still packed. After we dressed and were ready to go there were still people in the parking lot. All the bars and restaurants in Green Bay were packed. Nobody wanted the night to end.

GAME RESULT

For every player who was there, the memories come back in a flood. And everybody remembers something different.

For example, quarterback Lynn Dickey remembers the early-week taunt by a Redskins player who said the game would be a rout. That would prove impetus for not only Dickey, but for coach Bart Starr.

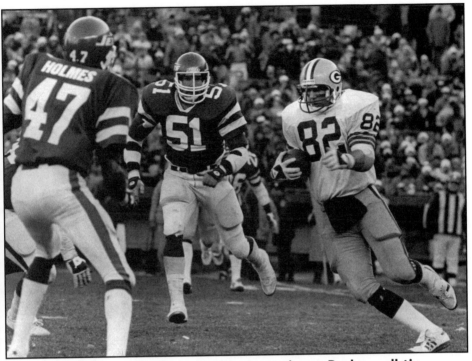

Paul Coffman's 322 receptions remains a Packers all-time record for tight ends. *Vernon J. Biever photo*

Coffman remembered no such comment and said he wouldn't have needed it anyway.

"I played hard no matter what," he said. "You're a professional and you should play hard every week. I went out and caught passes and ran over people."

Coffman needed no motivation because he had a first half that would be a season for some players. Paired up one on one against Redskins safety Curtis Jordan, Coffman ran wild and it was only after a halftime adjustment that Coffman was corralled. In the second quarter alone Coffman abused the Redskins' secondary, scoring on receptions of 36 and nine yards as the Packers built a 24-20 halftime lead.

The Redskins, with a fairly prolific offense of their own, appeared to take command in the third quarter and led 33-31, but another wave of scoring in the fourth quarter brought the game into the final minute when Jan Stenerud kicked a 20-yard field goal with 57 seconds left. And with this game, in which seven of the 16 scores came on drives of less than a minute, 57 seconds were several lifetimes. And that's exactly what happened as Washington moved from its 27 to the Green Bay 23 before Mark Moseley missed the 39-yard field goal on the final play.

WHAT BECAME OF PAUL COFFMAN?

He played eight seasons in Green Bay, and four of them were 8-8 campaigns. Today those numbers bemuse Coffman because it spoke to just how average the Green Bay teams were that he played for. But he always did his part. A free agent nobody from Kansas State, he went on to catch 322 passes, average 13 yards per catch and grab 39 touchdown passes. He remains the all-time leader among Packers tight ends, and it's a statistic he guards with pride.

He left the Packers after the 1985 season and spent two uneventful seasons with the Kansas City Chiefs and one more with the Vikings before he retired.

He bought 80 acres of land and put his college degree to work farming the land. But soon he decided to go to work for a friend of his, and today he's a salesman for Meyer Labs, a company that makes chemical cleaners. It allows him to stay around his family in the Kansas City area and offers him opportunities to do other things like coach freshman football at the local high school and watch his athletically gifted kids develop.

Two of his older sons, Chase and Carson, are superb high school football players in their own right. Chase is a wide receiver who has Big 12 schools keeping an eye on him, and Carson is a quarterback. His daughter, Camille, plays volleyball and basketball, and the youngest, Cameron, is a wrestler and basketball player.

Paul Coffman got out of his career everything he could have hoped for, and probably a little more.

"Just to be part of all that was great," he said.

CHAPTER 16

DON MAJKOWSKI

"Everything was clicking."

Name: Donald Vincent Majkowski
Birthdate: February 26, 1964
Hometown: Depew, New York
Current residence: Duluth, Georgia
Position: Quarterback
Height: 6-2
Playing weight: 203
Years: 1987-92
College: Virginia
Accomplishments: All-Pro 1989...Pro Bowl 1989.
The game: New Orleans Saints, September 17, 1989 at Lambeau Field

THE LIFE OF DON MAJKOWSKI

There was always that swashbuckling look to Don Majkowski. Blonde and blue-eyed with an ever-present smirk on his face that made it seem like he always knew a little bit more than you did. It was the perfect persona for the NFL quarterback, and he played to the hilt for as long as he could. And for one remarkable season, he was the best quarterback in the league, and that's more than a lot of players can claim.

He came out of the Buffalo suburbs of Depew, N.Y., relatively unknown. He went to Fork Union Academy in Virginia before enrolling at the University of Virginia, where he would offer enticing glimpses of what he would provide in later years for the Packers.

In fact, it was in his sophomore season with the Cavaliers that he engineered his first dramatic comeback. He led Virginia to the 1984 Peach Bowl against Purdue, but the Cavs found themselves trailing by 10 points at halftime.

In the third quarter, though, Majkowski pulled the offense together and capped a touchdown drive with a one-yard scoring run. After tying the game on a field goal, Majkowski spearheaded a fourth-quarter drive that led to a field goal and a 27-24 win.

He was a capable, if unimpressive, quarterback for a Virginia program still trying to find itself. He led the team in total offense for three straight seasons from 1984-86 and is still seventh all-time in school history in passing with 3,901 yards, 22 touchdowns and 29 interceptions.

He was one of those 'tweeners that either intrigue NFL pro personnel directors or send them screaming into the night. He had decent size, some running ability and a good enough arm to make the Packers decide to grab him in the 10th round of the 1987 draft. After all, the Packers had struggled through Randy Wright, Vince Ferragamo and Chuck Fusina in 1986, and those three managed to throw for barely 3,700 yards while heaving just 18 touchdowns and 27 interceptions. So it was no great gamble taking a project like Majkowski.

Don Majkowski. *Scott Halleran/Getty Images*

In 1987, Wright held out at the beginning of training camp; then the strike hit and the season finished with a 5-9-1 mark with Majkowski throwing for 875 yards and three scores.

In 1988, under new coach Lindy Infante, he battled with Wright again, and after leading the Packers to wins over New England and Minnesota, Majkowski seemed ready to take command. But the Packers went on a seven-game losing streak and scored just 53 points while they were at it. The disastrous conclusion led Infante to realize that he needed one guy in charge of his offense. In 1989, Majkowski would run the show, and oh, what a show it would be.

THE SETTING

It was a season unlike any the Packers had ever known before and, frankly, haven't seen since. Every game was a dance on the knife's edge, every play a study in human psychodrama. And in the middle of it all was Majkowski, the guy who was dubbed, wisely or not, "The Majic Man."

That season, the Packers won 10 games and came from behind to win seven of them. They also set an NFL record with four one-point wins. They won with the help of replay and they won with the help of stupid players on the other team. They won with incredible plays and with boneheaded maneuvers.

And everywhere there was Don Majkowski, blonde locks flowing and footballs flying. He was the quarterback who came practically from nowhere. In those days, Joe Montana and Randall Cunningham were king. They were quarterbacks who could make amazing plays out of nothing. Not some guy from Virginia whose name looked like a typographical error.

But that season no one was better than Majkowski at generating last-minute, jaw-dropping finishes that included one-point wins over New Orleans, Chicago and back-to-back wins over Tampa Bay and Minnesota.

Yet as incredible as the season was, the Packers were still the Packers. They closed the season with a flourish, beating the

Vikings and Bucs and closing with wins over the Bears and Cowboys. But sandwiched in the middle was a lackluster loss to the Kansas City Chiefs at Lambeau Field.

That loss would prove crushing as the Packers finished tied with the Vikings for the Central Division title. But the Vikings had a better division record overall, and these were still the days before the extra wild card berth. As a result Minnesota went to the playoffs and the Packers stayed home.

THE GAME OF MY LIFE
By Don Majkowski

Obviously I have one game that's more publicized and famous. That Bears game (the replay game on November 5) was the one everybody remembers, but before that there was the second game of the season against the New Orleans Saints. We came back from a 24-3 deficit against them. We had a rough first half and came back with a nice second half. I completed 18 consecutive passes to tie Lynn Dickey's record, and that was the first big comeback game of my career. That was the most memorable game of my career.

The first game of the season we had lost a tough, close game to Tampa Bay where I'd thrown a last-minute interception. So it was kind of a bad taste in my mouth spilling into the next week. And in the first half of the Saints game, we didn't have a lot of things going for us and the fans were getting on me pretty good. I had to suck it up and block everything out of my mind, and that's what made the game extra special.

At halftime, I spent all my time with [coach] Lindy [Infante] and he told me to just relax and play my game. We had a great game plan in the first half, but we had some unfortunate penalties that stalled drives. But if there was any game I can ever remember being in the zone and throwing the ball the best I ever had, it was definitely that game.

We had a perfect game plan, and Lindy did an unbelievable job of play calling. Everything was just there. I just had to get the ball to the open guy. Everything was clicking.

We had made a nice comeback and I think there was 1:22 left to play, and we needed a touchdown to win the game. During the course of that last drive, I got sacked and fumbled, and we ended up in that fourth-and-17 situation. I remember coming to the sideline and I asked Lindy what he wanted me to run. So we called a deep comeback on the far sideline. I remember throwing a perfect pass to Jeff Query. Fourth and 17 is a tough pass to complete. It was a great throw, and Jeff did a great job of keeping his feet inbounds. One official had called it out of bounds and then [referee] Ben Dreith overruled it.

Then on the touchdown to Sterling [Sharpe], it was designed to be a rub play. We thought they'd play man to man, so we sent Aubrey Mathews in motion to set up some interference and run Sterling's guy into coverage. But they played zone instead. Sterling did his slant route and got behind the guy. It wasn't designed that way, but he did a nice job. That was the icing on the cake.

That game set the tone for that whole season. It was a game that was kind of forgotten, but it was an unbelievable comeback. The Saints were on a roll in that game with [quarterback] Bobby Hebert and [running back] Dalton Hilliard. And to come back in the second half like that—it gave our team the confidence it needed. We were 4-12 the year before and we had lost our season opener, so that game was the start of it all in my opinion. That was the first year the job was mine.

GAME RESULT

The boos cascaded down on Majkowski and the Packers as they ran off the field at halftime. And, in truth, it had been an abysmal performance as New Orleans pushed the Packers all over the field.

But Majkowski, after a quick pep talk from Infante, was about to enter a realm he had never been before and would never see again.

The Packers scored on every possession in the second half as Brent Fullwood ran in from four yards out and Majkowski threw

In a season never to be duplicated, Don Majkowski threw for 4,318 yards and 27 touchdowns and was named to his only Pro Bowl in 1989. *Vernon J. Biever photo*

touchdown passes of three and 17 yards to tight end Ed West. Majkowski had completed his final two passes of the first half and then hit on 16 straight to begin the second half, tying a club record established by Lynn Dickey.

Even with all those fireworks, New Orleans appeared to wrap up the game when Morten Anderson kicked a field goal with 2:21 to play. But Majkowski wasn't done. He brought the Packers back down the field and, facing fourth and 17 from the Saints' 48, the end seemed to have come.

But Majkowski found Jeff Query, a tiny, speedy wide receiver from little Millikin University, on the sideline for a 23-yard catch. The officials did indeed confer after one said it was out of bounds. But the catch was ruled good and the drive continued. Majkowski hit Query two more times down to the Saints' three when Majkowski connected with Sharpe for the game-winning score with 1:26 to play. For the game Majkowski completed 25 of 32 passes for 354 yards with Sharpe catching eight passes and Query four.

It was the start of a season few would ever forget. Majkowski went on to throw for an astounding 4,318 yards and 27 touchdowns and earn a Pro Bowl berth.

WHAT BECAME
OF DON MAJKOWSKI?

This was the same season, of course, that featured the infamous replay game against the Bears when Majkowski, seemingly over the line of scrimmage, threw a winning touchdown pass to Sharpe.

First ruled a penalty, the official consulted replays and said he was not over the line of scrimmage and ruled it a touchdown.

"That Bears game, personally, I didn't have a good game statistically," Majkowski said. "But team-wise, it was the biggest team win I was ever associated with. What was so rewarding in that game is that they were so good. Talk about a flair for the dramatic."

But the magic didn't last. In 1990, Majkowski held out for 45 days at the start of training camp in a bitter contract dispute. He returned at the beginning of the season, but it was never the same.

He did engineer another comeback win early in the season, but on November 18 he suffered a shoulder injury that affected him the rest of the season. In 1991 the injuries continued and the Packers continued to fade. Infante was fired and Mike Holmgren was hired, and along with him came a young hotshot quarterback named Brett Favre.

Though Majkowski began 1992 as the starter, it was clear Holmgren saw the future was with Favre. That future began on September 20, 1992, against Cincinnati when Majkowski was knocked out with an ankle injury. Favre took over, led the Packers to a last-second win and never left the lineup.

Majkowski left Green Bay after that season and went to Indianapolis for two years and Detroit for two more. But he never recaptured the brilliance he had known in 1989.

"I finally had to retire because of that ankle injury," he said. "It kind of lingered for a couple of years."

In fact, Majkowski went through some difficult years following his retirement. That ankle required three different surgeries over three years.

"I had teams calling me, and it was difficult," he said. "That was the frustrating thing. I was just 34 and I was in great shape. But I had tried to come back way too soon after the 1996 season."

He left football and went to work with a friend as an area manager in computer data storage.

"I absolutely hated it and was bored out of my mind," Majkowski said.

Then he met Mark Benson, who suggested to Majkowski he team up with him in real estate investment. Now they own Hotlanta Homebuyers in suburban Atlanta. Majkowski has other irons in the fire as well, though he says now nothing is definite.

CHAPTER 17

BART STARR

"Everyone knew exactly what was at stake."

Name: Bryan Bartlett Starr
Birthdate: January 9, 1934
Hometown: Montgomery, Alabama
Current residence: Birmingham, Alabama
Position: Quarterback
Height: 6-1
Playing weight: 190
Years: 1956-71
College: Alabama
Accomplishments: Inducted into Pro Football Hall of Fame in 1977...Named to Pro Bowl 1960-62 and 1966...League MVP in 1966...MVP in Super Bowl I and II...Inducted into Packer Hall of Fame in 1977...Highest quarterback rating in NFL playoff history.
The game: Dallas Cowboys, December 31, 1967 at Lambeau Field.

THE LIFE OF BART STARR

Before he became one of the NFL's all-time great quarterbacks and perhaps the most enduring figure as a Green Bay Packer, Bart Starr was just like everybody else. It might have seemed as though he had sprung fully formed and ready to play quarterback at the highest levels, but that was far from the case.

There was a stretch as a youngster when Starr went almost three years without seeing his father whose National Guard unit was called up for WWII. Perhaps, those were the years when he developed the quiet confidence and steely resolve that would one day make him a Hall of Famer.

Starr grew up in Montgomery, Alabama, where as a junior at Sidney Lanier High School he took over as starting quarterback when the other quarterback broke his leg. As a senior, Starr was an All-State selection, and when it came time to choose a college, he selected Alabama.

He seemed on his way to a superb college career when, as a sophomore, he led the Crimson Tide to the Cotton Bowl (a loss to Rice). But the upward movement did not continue. As a junior, he was plagued by back problems, and with a change in coaching staff the next year, Starr and numerous other seniors watched from the sidelines as Alabama staggered in with a 0-10 record.

Despite those disappointments, Starr hoped the NFL would still take a look, and in 1956, the Packers, coming off a 6-6 season and in need of a quarterback, took Starr in the 17th round of a draft that in those days went 30 rounds.

In his first three pro seasons, Starr did nothing to make anyone think he'd be the answer to the Packers' prayers. He completed barely half of his passes and threw only 13 touchdowns while throwing 25 interceptions and the Packers won only eight games in his first three years.

But all of that was about to change.

Bart Starr. *AP/WWP*

THE SETTING

Bart Starr remembered his first encounter with Vince Lombardi, but only after he learned the obscure New York Giants offensive line coach would become the Packers' new head coach in 1959.

"I didn't know who he was until recognizing a picture of him in one of the Green Bay papers," he said. "I recognized his face immediately because the year before in a preseason game at Fenway Park, we had scored a touchdown and, just as it was at Milwaukee County Stadium, the benches were on the same side of the field. While jogging off after holding for the extra point and going past the Giants' bench, I see this guy who is ranting and raving at defensive players for the Giants. Then I recognized him. To show you his aggressiveness and intensity, he was yelling at the defensive players and he was the offensive line coach."

Starr got a better idea of what the future held in his first meeting with Lombardi.

"He looked us in the eye and said, 'Gentlemen, we are always going to relentlessly chase perfection, knowing full well we will not catch it because nothing is perfect. In the process we will catch excellence.' He paused and said, 'I'm not remotely interested in being just good.' We knew immediately there would be a change. I called my wife back in Alabama and said, 'Honey, we're going to begin to win.' It was an absolutely wonderful experience."

Lombardi understood immediately that Starr's strength was intelligence and poise and the ability to make decisions at the right time, and he played to those strengths. Starr never threw more than 295 passes in a season, but he also never completed fewer than 52 percent of his passes, either, and that was in Lombardi's first season.

Starr choreographed NFL titles in 1961 and 1962 and again in 1965 and 1966, when he was named the NFL MVP when he threw for 2,257 yards, completed 62 percent of his passes and threw only three interceptions.

THE GAME OF MY LIFE
By Bart Starr

Foremost in my mind is the Ice Bowl because of its significance on several levels. Football fans remember the weather, which was no doubt a key element. What some observers forget is that we were a team competing for our third consecutive NFL championship and our fifth title in the decade of the 1960s, yet we were playing with several starters on the injured list. That's what stands out in my mind even more than the weather.

There are a couple of things about the game that people may not remember. The change in the weather from Saturday to Sunday was one. When we went out for our light Saturday workout, the field was in great condition. The temperature was zero, but there was no wind. The problem developed overnight as a cold front moved in and led to a damaged heating system under the field. At kickoff the footing was tolerable, but as the game progressed it deteriorated to the point where we were skating rather than running.

In addition, few football experts wrote about the quality of the Cowboys' team. They were talented, physical and well prepared. We were more experienced, but they had earned the right to be there. Despite the brutal weather, the Cowboys nearly matched us that day, and it took every bit of creativity and determination on our part to win the game.

As we ran onto the field to start what would be our last drive, I stepped into the huddle and looked into the eyes of my teammates. I knew instantly that nothing needed to be said regarding the importance of that opportunity. Everyone knew exactly what was at stake and what would be required.

I do not believe we can single out any play as the most important of that drive, because the very nature of a game-winning drive is that every play is crucial. I prefer to focus on the tremendous contribution from a couple of players who never received enough credit. We had a dedicated, committed group of guys who were also very bright. For example, Donny Anderson, our halfback, observed that the linebacker covering him was dropping off into deeper than normal coverage, which meant I could safely pass the ball to him for modest but steady gains. Chuck Mercein, our fullback, noted that the linebacker covering him was staying too far toward the middle of the field, which allowed us to achieve a large gain on a relatively simple swing pass.

Equally important was a play we planned for but had not yet used. We waited until it was perfect for that drive. I handed the ball to Chuck Mercein on what was called an "influence" play. If you were looking at the back of our offensive line, our left guard pulled to the right. (Cowboys defensive tackle) Bob Lilly was opposite him and charging at an angle almost parallel to the line, which meant that we could not block him cleanly. We decided to use Lilly's tremendous quickness and anticipation to our advantage. We pulled our guard, Gale Gillingham, to the right, hoping that Lilly would try to beat him to the point of attack. This would take Lilly out of the play, which was going to be run in the spot

One of the most famous photos in sports history: Bart Starr sneaking into the end zone to beat the Cowboys in the "Ice Bowl." *AP/WWP*

where he originally lined up. This was a risky call, but I believed the time had come to try it, as the adrenaline was running full tilt and Lilly would likely try to make a decisive play for their defense, which he had done so many times.

There was a second aspect to this play, without which we could not have succeeded. If Lilly took himself out of the intended hole, we knew that the Cowboys' defensive end, George Andre, would cover the area unless our left tackle, Bob Skoronski, could cut him off. I asked Bob if he could make that block and he said yes. That was all I needed to hear.

The play was a huge success, the highlight of the drive. Mercein gained eight crucial yards, and if the field had been better he might have scored. Had that occurred, the quarterback sneak on the goal line would have been moot. It was the most memorable play I ever called. It perfectly illustrated how important it was for every player to execute his block, because if Skoronski had failed to cut off Andre, we would have achieved only a one- or two-yard gain. In my opinion, Skoronski should be in the Hall of Fame. He was an outstanding offensive tackle. Had he not been overshadowed by his teammate, Forrest Gregg, one of the best tackles ever to play the game, he would already be in Canton.

That game certainly helped our spirit. We'd had the toughest year imaginable. We were two-time defending NFL champions, badly banged up, and everybody wanted an extra piece of us. Each team was at its very best when we played them.

GAME RESULT

Anyone with even a passing interest in pro football knows the details of this one. It was, perhaps, the game that turned the NFL from a sport America enjoyed to a sport America devoured.

There were so many subplots coming into play from the weather—which was 13 degrees below zero—to the significance of the game to the competition that saw the reigning kings, the Packers, facing the new rising power in the Dallas Cowboys.

And the fact is, the Cowboys played well enough to beat the Packers despite the weather conditions.

Early on, the Packers were in command, taking a 14-0 lead on two Starr-to-Boyd Dowler touchdowns—one of eight yards and the other of 46. But the Cowboys climbed back in when the Cowboys' Willie Townes sacked Starr and he fumbled, and George Andrie picked up the ball for the touchdown. After another Packers fumble, Danny Villanueva kicked a 20-yard field goal and Green Bay led 14-10 at halftime.

The weather grew even colder and the field hardened, and the game became a study in survival as much as anything else.

After a scoreless third quarter, the Cowboys stunned the Packers on the first play of the fourth quarter when halfback Dan Reeves took a pitch and threw 50 yards for the score to Lance Rentzel.

The Packers got the ball back with 4:54 to play and the ball on the Green Bay 32-yard line. The rest is the stuff of history. Starr completed key passes to Dowler, Donny Anderson and Chuck Mercein. Then Mercein, on the "give" play touted by Starr, rolled up the middle for an 18-yard gain to the Cowboys' three. Then it was third down from 1 with 13 seconds to play.

"I asked the linemen if they could get their footing for one more wedge play, and they said yes," Starr said.

He called a timeout and went to the sideline to confer with Lombardi.

"I told him the linemen could get their footing but the running backs were having trouble getting their footing and that I was upright and could shuffle my feet and get in on the wedge play," Starr said. "Lombardi said, 'Well, run it, and let's the get hell out of here.' And I went back to the huddle chuckling."

Starr wedged in over center Ken Bowman and right guard Jerry Kramer, and the game took its frozen place in history. Again, lost in all of that was the fact that the Packers still had to play the Oakland Raiders in Super Bowl II in Miami. But, in almost an afterthought, the Packers prevailed 33-14 and Starr was the MVP.

WHAT BECAME OF BART STARR?

He was around so long that many Packers fans could hardly imagine a time when Bart Starr wasn't the quarterback. After Super Bowl II, though, changes started to come.

Lombardi left the sidelines and moved in solely as general manager, leaving his top assistant Phil Bengston as the new coach. But it was an uncomfortable arrangement at best, and after one season away from coaching, Lombardi left Green Bay to coach the Washington Redskins. A year later, he was dead of cancer.

Meanwhile Bengston had no hope of escaping Lombardi's considerable shadow, and the Packers stumbled. Starr did complete a career-best 64 percent of his passes in 1968, but the Packers missed the playoffs with a 6-7-1 record. He remained the starter two more years and played four games in 1971 before retiring in training camp prior to the 1972 season.

He came back in 1972 to help coach a new batch of Packers quarterbacks before leaving after a year to do some TV work for CBS. Starr had been in the automobile business since 1969, and after his television stint, he devoted his full attention to that.

But the NFL called again, and when the Packers asked him to take over as head coach in 1975, even though he had no head coaching experience, he couldn't refuse. He lasted nine seasons, his teams went 52-76-3, and he was fired after the 1983 season. It's a period in his life he politely chooses not to talk about.

After living for a time in Phoenix, where he was part of a group that tried unsuccessfully to get an NFL expansion franchise, he moved back to Birmingham, where he is now in the health care real estate business. Starr is chairman of the services arm of HealthCare Realty Trust, and though the publicly traded company is based in Nashville, he's able to stay in Birmingham with his family.

"It's been an absolutely joyful experience," he said.

As for his years with the Packers, they remain some of the best of his life.

"It's indescribable," he said. "It's a blessing and a thrill you'll treasure the rest of your life. Cherry and I will always consider Green Bay our adopted home. We lived 31 years in Wisconsin and it was fabulous."

CHAPTER 18

MARV FLEMING

"This was going to be easy."

Name: Marvin Xavier Fleming
Birthdate: January 2, 1942
Hometown: Compton, California
Current residence: Marina de Ray, California
Position: Tight end
Height: 6-4
Playing weight: 232
Years: 1963-69
College: University of Utah
Accomplishments: Packers' 11th-round draft pick in 1963...Part of what at the time was a record five Super Bowl teams (two in Green Bay and three in Miami).
The game: Baltimore Colts, October 27, 1963 at Memorial Stadium

THE LIFE OF MARV FLEMING

There are some guys who just happen to be in the right place at the right time. And in his pro career, Marv Fleming was one of those guys. He never shied away from pushing the envelope, from doing things that other guys couldn't, or wouldn't, do. Maybe that's why a kid from inner-city Los Angeles decided to play college football at a place like the University of Utah, a world away from where he came from.

But he learned then what it was like to get along with everybody. In 1963, the Packers were already well into their era as one of the NFL's most dominant franchises. They had already won world titles in 1961 and 1962, so there were precious few openings on a team that would go on to win three more titles. Still, the Packers needed a backup for Ron Kramer at tight end, and in a draft that also produced starters Dave Robinson, Tom Brown and Lionel Aldridge, the Packers took an athletic and sometimes outspoken tight end from Utah in the 11th round. He would prove the perfect complement to a team that was already loaded.

THE SETTING

Green Bay remains, by a wide margin, the smallest city in the nation to host an NFL franchise. It is part of the allure that is the Green Bay Packers that a city of 90,000 not only has an NFL franchise but can be as consistently strong as it's been the last decade or so.

So just imagine the Green Bay of the early 1960s. It was even smaller, even more insular, and if players live in the proverbial fishbowl today, they lived in a coffee cup back then. Everybody knew the Packers, and the joke, though it really wasn't all that funny, was when a black man was seen walking through all-white Green Bay, he had to be a Packers player.

But there was little racial tension, if any, on those Packers teams because they knew that anyone who could help them win

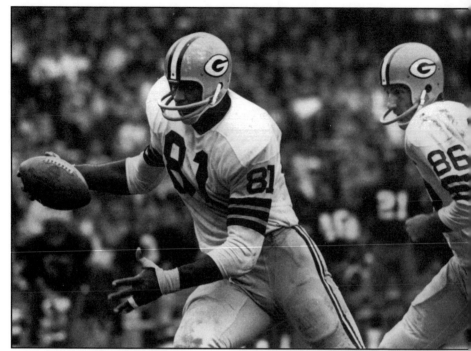

Marv Fleming. *Vernon J. Biever photo*

would have a place in the huddle. And Lombardi wouldn't abide such dissension anyway.

"On Vince Lombardi's teams, there were no racial overtones," Fleming said. "If there were—boom—they were out there. But that didn't mean we didn't have to be careful. I remember one of the players told Lombardi one night that I was out with a white girl, so Lombardi called me into his office the next day. He said, 'Marvin, I know you were popular at Utah and we like you here, but you have to be discreet.' I said, 'Is that all?' and he said, 'Yeah,' and I said, 'OK.' Everybody was on equal terms with Lombardi."

In fact, Fleming would go on to develop a strong and enduring friendship with his fellow tight end, Ron Kramer, a Kansas boy who played at Michigan. It's a friendship as strong today as it was 40 years ago to the point that they still talk three times a week.

"If it wasn't for Ron Kramer, I wouldn't be the football player I am today," Fleming said. "I idolized him. I saw what type of football player he was, I saw how he blocked, how he caught passes and what his motivation was."

But in 1963, Fleming still had to earn his stripes—not because of his skin color but because as a unit, the Packers knew what they had. Every player had a role and did it to the best of their ability. If one player broke down, the whole team could. That's why Fleming was greeted so skeptically that first time on the field. But once you passed your test with teammates, there was never another question about your ability.

THE GAME OF MY LIFE
By Marv Fleming

My biggest game was when I played in Baltimore. [Starting tight end] Ron Kramer was hurt and here I am on the sidelines with [backup running back] Elijah Pitts and I hear my name, "Fleming, Fleming." And I think to myself, "Oh no, this is not special teams unit time." I'm so excited I almost run out there without my helmet. I'm thinking "Ron's hurt? Ron never gets hurt." But I ran out there on the field and we're playing the Baltimore Colts. One of my good friends was [Colts All-Pro tight] John Mackey, and I always thought I was as good as he was.

So I run into the huddle and the veterans look at me, and one of the veteran guys said, "Marvin, you better know the plays, because if you don't, I'm going to kick your butt." I said, "You do your job and I'll do mine," and that's when everybody in the huddle said, "Whoa."

Several plays later I caught a big pass that set up a touchdown, and after that I guess you could say I was invited to the party. I won their confidence.

The Packers had already won [NFL titles] once or twice before I'd gotten there, and it's true what they say that you take on the mentality of your peers. That's what I did. I was a winner already. Being with the Green Bay Packers, it instilled winningness in me, and that goes on today. Being with Herb Adderley, Willie Wood and Bart Starr, having seen all these guys on TV, I wanted to be just like them. I wanted to be a winner.

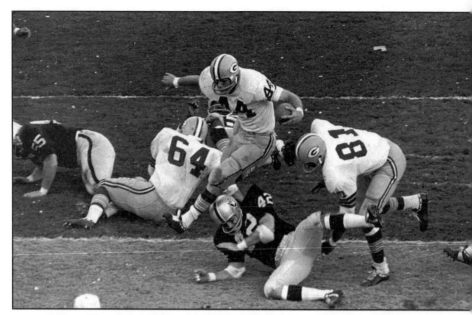

Marv Fleming (81) played in two Super Bowls with Green Bay and three more in Miami—winning four of them—and earned a special place in NFL history. *AP/WWP*

But that first catch was the highlight—when you get that first call. A lot of times when that happens, you get flustered. But I caught that huge pass and I threw the ball on the ground and said, "This is going to be easy."

GAME RESULT

The Packers did well just to get out of this game alive. This was a team that had chalked up two straight NFL titles, but they were in a war for a third straight with the Chicago Bears (who would end winning the Western Division by a half-game over the Packers). But coming up quickly were the Baltimore Colts, a team that had dipped since its heyday in the late 1950s but was starting to rebuild a powerhouse.

In 1963, the Packers had already beaten the Colts in Green Bay and needed this one to at least stay close to the Bears. But it wouldn't be easy.

Heading into the game in Baltimore, starting quarterback Bart Starr didn't play after breaking a hand the week before in St. Louis. Also absent was halfback Tom Moore. Then early in the game, All-Pro tight end Ron Kramer injured his leg and didn't return. Those were three key spots that required three key replacements, and somehow, the Packers muddled through.

John Roach, a journeyman quarterback from SMU, got the start in place of Starr and was efficient enough, completing nine of 20 passes for 156 yards. Elijah Pitts, who would take over as a starter in later years, stepped in for Moore and was solid as well, with 74 yards on 10 carries.

And then there was the rookie Fleming, something of an unknown who had done little up to that stage of the season except play on special teams. But he made his mark on this day with three catches for 51 yards, including an 11-yard touchdown catch in the second quarter that put the Packers up 17-3 at halftime.

The Colts did come back to tie the game at 20-20 with six minutes to play, but Green Bay turned the tide two minutes later when Willie Davis and Jerry Norton blocked a field goal. Pitts then ran 34 yards for a touchdown, and Jim Taylor scored again later to seal the 34-20 win.

Fleming caught only four more passes the rest of that season, though that was hardly the point. He had been called on to do a job and he did it, and everything else would take care of itself.

WHAT BECAME OF MARV FLEMING?

Ron Kramer played through the 1964 season in Green Bay before family considerations convinced him to sign with the hometown Detroit Lions. That meant the starting tight end job belonged to Fleming. Before Kramer left, though, he imparted all the knowledge and wisdom he could to the young replacement.

And over the next five seasons, Fleming would become a solid, dependable tight end who could block and catch and get downfield. His best season in Green Bay was 1966 when he caught 31 passes. He caught 109 passes and 12 touchdowns in his seven seasons in Green Bay before coach Phil Bengston traded him to Miami for wide receiver Jack Clancy. Fleming didn't know it at the time, but he went from a declining NFL power to a rising force.

He became the blocking tight end for a surging Miami Dolphins running game, and he would go to three more Super Bowls in 1971, 1972 and 1973 for the Dolphins—winning two of them. He is part of the undefeated 1972 Dolphins team that still holds celebrations when the last team in the current NFL season loses.

Actually, Fleming has made something of a career since he retired selling that 17-0 Dolphins' season in 1972.

"One night I said to myself that I can sell this idea," he said. "I can sell the perfect season. So I started calling a lot of the players and they liked the idea. I got $1,000 and I bought $1,000 worth of footballs and jerseys and helmets. We sign them and we have a reunion and everybody became part of the company. I became chairman of the 1972 Perfect Season Team."

And every year, when the last unbeaten team falls, all the team members celebrate their longstanding accomplishment.

"Last year when the Bengals played the [unbeaten] Chiefs, I couldn't watch," Fleming said. "But the Bengals ended up winning and I went outside and screamed and all my neighbors could hear me."

Fleming is also a motivational speaker, and most of his talks are about growing up and the influence Vince Lombardi had on his life.

"No one leaves," he said of audiences.

CHAPTER 19

JIM CARTER

"I did my job well."

Name: James Charles Carter
Birthdate: October 18, 1948
Hometown: St. Paul, Minnesota
Current residence: Eleva, Wisconsin
Position: Linebacker
Height: 6-3
Playing weight: 235
Years: 1970-78
College: University of Minnesota
Accomplishments: Pro Bowl 1973
The game: Philadelphia Eagles, October 25, 1970 at Milwaukee County Stadium

THE LIFE OF JIM CARTER

Jim Carter is still outrunning his demons. After all these years away from football, the pressure, the anger and the uncertainty, he is finally at peace with himself and his turbulent, exhilarating years with the Green Bay Packers.

"I'm a recovering person," he said. "I quit drinking 21 years ago and I've had some other addictions. And while most people will tell you addictions go back to childhood, the experience I had with the Nitschke situation exacerbated the situation. I was ill-equipped emotionally to deal with it. I probably didn't have a strong enough self-image."

Carter was likely a ticking bomb from his earliest years as high school star from South St. Paul, Minnesota. He decided to attend the hometown University of Minnesota, where he was a terrific fullback, earning All-Big Ten honors. He was also an exceptional hockey player and was drafted by the Minnesota Fighting Saints of the World Hockey Association. But there was no doubt in his mind where his future was.

He wanted to play in the NFL, and it had been his hope that if, and when, he was drafted that he'd get the opportunity to be a running back again. Those hopes died quickly, however, when the Packers made Carter their third-round pick in 1970 and immediately moved him to linebacker.

"I thought I was a pretty good running back in college," he said. "I was hoping to get a chance at running back, but I never played a down."

That's because these Packers of a new decade were reformulating and seeking a new identity. The players from those championship days of the 1960s were retiring or being traded, and new blood had to step in to fill the vacuum.

One player from the golden years was still doggedly holding on and still playing good football. Ray Nitschke had been a force at middle linebacker for the Packers since 1958. He had already been a three-time All-Pro, a Pro Bowler and was voted to the NFL's

Jim Carter. *Vernon J. Biever photo*

All-50 Year Team. His ticket to the Hall of Fame had already been bought and paid for.

But in 1971, Nitschke still wasn't ready to move aside. He was convinced he still had plenty of good football left in him and that, if he didn't, it was up to the next young stud to beat him out.

In 1970, Carter had stepped in for one legend when he took over for the injured Robinson. In 1971, new coach Dan Devine was impressed enough with Carter's play to move him into the middle linebacker spot in training camp. The promotion should have made Carter ecstatic. Instead, it was just the beginning of a nightmare that simply would not end.

THE SETTING

Nitschke was a proud man who didn't feel his job should be handed to a second-year guy. And Packers fans, who had grown to love Nitschke's relentless, take-no-prisoners style on the field, were angry that a kid had taken his place. So every time Carter took the field, he was greeted with a torrent of boos.

"The booing wasn't about who I was as a person; it was about replacing somebody like Nitschke," Carter said.

He understands that now. He didn't then.

"It bothered me so much that I drank more, smoked more grass, got laid more," he said. "I knew I wasn't emotionally or psychologically prepared. And once it started, it was tough the whole time. It never got any better."

And Nitschke didn't do much to help his young replacement. There would be times during games when Nitschke would be on the sidelines and would start to stretch as though he was getting ready to enter the game. When fans saw that, they went nuts. But instead Carter remained, infuriating fans even more. Nitschke finally retired after the 1972 season.

"At first it wasn't about me, and then it was about me, because I didn't handle it very well," Carter said. "I had a TV show in 1972 and there was this question-and-answer period where this woman asked me if I ever thought I'd be good enough to fill the shoes of

Ray Nitschke," he said. "Now I'd had a few drinks before the show and I had heard enough of this. So I told her to go to hell. I just reacted badly. In 1973 I was an All-Pro. I wasn't at Nitschke's or Dick Butkus's level, but to be a middle linebacker starting in the NFL, you have to be fairly good. I was good enough to play, good enough to be a starter, good enough to be a team captain for four years. But I wasn't Nitschke. Plus our teams weren't that good."

THE GAME OF MY LIFE
By Jim Carter

The game I really remember that year was when we played Philadelphia and we played them in Milwaukee. The Eagles had a tight end named Steve Zabel, and he went on to become a linebacker and became a very, very good player. But at that time he was a tight end and our staring left linebacker, Dave Robinson, had torn his Achilles tendon and they started me at outside linebacker.

Now Robby was such a great player even late in his career. I never saw anybody do such a great job on tight ends as he did. He was an artist. I tried to emulate him, but I was nowhere near the player he was. I was told in that game that my job was to stand Zabel up. I knew Zabel was tough and strong and I was pretty successful at doing that in that game. I did my job well. I think then I knew after that game that I could play in this league. I think [defensive line coach] Dave Hanner and [new head coach in 1971] Dan Devine, probably thought the same thing, and maybe that's why they put me in the middle after that. I did a pretty good job in that game and that helped them make that decision. I don't remember if I made any tackles in that game, but I felt I could control him and that's what they wanted.

GAME RESULT

Even if the 1970 Packers weren't the powerhouse of two years earlier, fans still had expectations. And when the Packers skidded to an ugly 30-17 victory over the winless Eagles, it was further evidence that the good old days were gone for good.

Carter did indeed play well and held Steve Zabel without a catch. He had four tackles overall and proved to any objective observer that he was a linebacker to be taken seriously.

The Packers jumped on the Eagles quickly when Doug Hart returned an interception 76 yards for a touchdown and Green Bay went on to force four other Philadelphia turnovers.

There was very little remarkable about a midseason game between the now average Packers and the hopeless Eagles. Bart Starr, nearing the end of his career as well, threw for 129 yards, and the Packers' defense held the Eagles to 241 total yards.

WHAT BECAME OF JIM CARTER?

What should have been the crowning moment of his life—playing middle linebacker for the storied Packers—was instead, quite literally, a hell on earth for Carter.

Even after Nitschke's retirement and his plea to fans to take it easy on Carter, the fans never let up. Certainly Carter's surly, sullen attitude didn't help, but chances are anyone replacing a legend would have struggled just as much.

"I talked too much and drank too much," Carter said. "What could have been a great experience turned into a pretty sour experience for me. But that's how I handled it."

He has come to grips with his years in Green Bay and many fans today who remember him apologize for the awful treatment he received. But even though he has lived just across the state since he retired, he has yet to return to watch a game or for an annual player reunion.

"I've always been afraid to go back," he said. "If there are 60,000 people there and there are 59,900 cheering, I'd only hear the boos. I've had teammates tell me to come back, but it's too tough on my emotional makeup."

After retiring after the 1978 season, Carter took a year off to recuperate. His father and brother owned automobile dealerships in Eau Claire, and Carter decided to go that route. He expanded his dealership into Ford, General Motors, Chevrolet, Audi and others, and he built one of the largest dealerships in the region.

"I actually had too much," Carter said.

He sold the dealerships two years ago, and though he still dabbles in real estate, he is all but retired to a large spread in rural Eau Claire, where he and his family raise llamas.

"I'm more a landlord now," he said.

He understands, at least a little, why his years in Green Bay were so difficult and, if he could, he would do a lot of things differently.

"It's hard to complain much about it because most people would give their right arm to play in the NFL," he said. "I know that now."

CHAPTER 20

LARRY McCARREN

"We did what we did best."

Name: Laurence Anthony McCarren
Birthdate: November 9, 1951
Hometown: Park Forest, Illinois
Current residence: Green Bay, Wisconsin
Position: Center
Height: 6-3
Playing weight: 240
Years: 1973-84
College: University of Illinois
Accomplishments: Pro Bowl 1982 and 1983...All-Pro 1982...
Inducted into Packers Hall of Fame in 1992.
The game: Washington Redskins, October 17, 1983, Lambeau
Field

Larry McCarren. *Vernon J. Biever photo*

THE LIFE OF LARRY McCARREN

He is one of the great overachievers on a franchise where there have been many.

Even back in the early to mid-1970s when McCarren was slamming away at rival defensive tackles, he was considered under-sized for the position. But through doggedness and an innate toughness, he battled through all the odds and earned one of the great nicknames in Packers history: "Rock." Its genesis was simple enough. It was awarded to him for his rock-steady play, game in and game out.

Over a 12-year career he played in 162 games, and even when he shouldn't have played, he did. In 1980, for example, he had a hernia operation during training camp. He had all but recovered but was far from 100 percent when the season opened. Still, coach Bart Starr put him in just to keep his consecutive games started streak alive. Then he'd remove him. But after the first play, McCarren waved off his replacement and he played the entire game.

He played through a broken hand and, in one especially bizarre incident, his family was overcome by carbon monoxide fumes one morning, but he played later that day. And, oh yes, he played center in the NFL at the relatively puny weight of 240 pounds.

"He's the toughest player I've ever been around," quarterback Lynn Dickey said.

THE SETTING

McCarren joined the Packers at what could charitably be called the beginning of the franchise's dark ages. A relative-ly obscure 12th-round draft pick, he labored on the old taxi squad his first season before taking over the starting center job from another holdover from the golden era, Ken Bowman, in 1974. He would hold the job for the next 11 years.

But in that time, he would see some of the most mediocre football this franchise could produce. In his 12 seasons, the Packers reached the playoffs once, in 1982. He didn't see a .500 mark until 1978 when the Packers went 8-7-1, and while hope always blossomed every season, it was always crushing disappointment by end.

The optimism seemed justified late in McCarren's career when, after earning the strike-shortened playoff berth in 1982, the Packers welcomed back most of the team in 1983.

But while the offense was more that adequate, the defense was a shambles. Inconsistency plagued the team from beginning to end, and often it was because the defense could be counted on to collapse spectacularly. The Packers' final playoff gasp ended with a regular season-ending loss to the Bears.

In 1984, Forrest Gregg replaced Bart Starr and managed to carve out an 8-8 record, including three straight wins to end the season. But McCarren missed those final three games with a pinched nerve in his neck.

THE GAME OF MY LIFE
By Larry McCarren

It was a special night for an offensive player, and I remember a couple of things leading up to it. We had a big-play offense that year and we could light it up, but we didn't have much on defense. In previous games we had tried to slow the game down to help the defense, and that just wasn't our offense.

So Bill Meyer, the offensive line coach, came up to us the week before the game and said enough of that ball-control stuff. [Offensive coordinator] Bob Schnelker said, "The defense is just going to have to fend for itself. We're cutting loose." And we ran everything we had. Overall we played really well. We just said to heck with that ball control and we did what we did best. We went for home runs and got huge chunks of yardage. It was one of those games that whoever got the ball last was the one who's going to win the thing.

Then it came to the final field goal attempt, and Schnelker, after orchestrating that offensive explosion, couldn't bear to watch. He just turned his back on the field. That missed field goal was probably the highlight of all the highlights.

You could look at that one as a team effort. The blocking was there, the coaching was there, the play-calling was there. These were the defending Super Bowl champs and we beat them. You have to look at it as an overall team effort.

It was, comparatively speaking, a very memorable moment in Packers history. It was a good opponent and it was on Monday night. Walking off the field, I've seen pictures, and I remember how great it felt to win a game like that.

GAME RESULT

Much has been written about the unforgettable offensive display in this game. There were 771 total yards gained and 95 points scored, and the two teams combined to run for 254 yards.

But what is often forgotten is the play of the Packers offensive line that protected Lynn Dickey from what was considered a fearsome Redskins pass rush. McCarren, of course, anchored the line at center, but it was also a line that had to be rebuilt for the Redskins game.

Regular right guard Leotis Harris was hurt, and that forced normal right tackle, Greg Koch, over to Harris's spot. To replace Koch, the Packers signed Charlie Getty. Karl Swanke was the left tackle and Dave Dreschler was the left guard. Those five kept Dickey vertical most of the night despite a pass rush that featured the NFL's most feared rusher, Dexter Mann, and massive tackle Dave Butz. It's a tidbit from the game few acknowledge.

"You don't ring up that kind of yardage without someone blocking some folks," McCarren said.

Dickey was sacked three times, but more importantly, he threw for 387 yards in a game that, more than 20 years later, is still regarded as a classic.

To McCarren, who had suffered through his share of awful seasons and even worse games, the only reason it became significant is because the Packers won.

"Up until that point, it was just a game where, yeah, we were moving the football," he said. "But until we won, that's when it became special. The end result made it special. We went to Atlanta later in the season and we lost 40 something to 40 something [47-41] and that wasn't anything special. This was special. Everything worked."

WHAT BECAME
OF LARRY McCARREN?

After 162 games and 12 seasons, even Larry McCarren couldn't defy time. He was the only center many Packers fans had ever known, and while he wasn't the most high-profile of players, his presence was still comforting. He had been there. He knew what to do. And you could count on him.

But his streak of consecutive games finally ended at the end of 1984 season when a pinched nerve forced him out of the lineup. He tried to come back in 1985, but it wasn't to be, and he retired during training camp, ending one of the most remarkable careers in Packers history was over.

But he wouldn't stray far. He moved immediately into television work and he has been mainstay at WFRV-TV in Green Bay, where he has earned numerous awards. In 1995, he also moved into the radio booth with veteran announcers Jim Irwin and Max McGee. In 1999, when Wayne Larrivee was hired as the new play-by-play announcer, McCarren took over as the sole color analyst. And, just like in his playing days, he's been there ever since.

CHAPTER 21

BRETT FAVRE

"I really thought I was done."

Name: Brett Lorenzo Favre
Born: October 10, 1969
Hometown: Kiln, Mississippi
Current residence: Hattiesburg, Mississippi
Position: Quarterback
Height: 6-2
Playing weight: 224
Years: 1992-present
College: Southern Mississippi
Accomplishments: Three-time NFL MVP 1995-97...Eight-time Pro Bowler 1992-93, 1995-97 and 2001-03...All-Pro 1995-97...Played in 208 consecutive games through the 2003 season, an NFL record for quarterbacks...Led NFL in touchdown passes four times...Second all-time in touchdown passes with 346 in the regular season...Has thrown for more than 50,000 yards (including playoffs)...Named *USA Today* "Toughest Athlete in Sports" and *Men's Journal* "Toughest Guy in America" in 2004.
The game: Minnesota Vikings, November 2, 2003 at the Metrodome

THE LIFE OF BRETT FAVRE

It has been a journey of wondrous myth, remarkable talent and head-shaking luck for Brett Favre, and it all came together to the point where he is now the most identifiable Packer in the team's long and storied history.

Every Packers fan, and even those who aren't necessarily Packers fans, have a favorite Brett Favre story. They remember a game he played or a pass he threw or a play he made that no one should make but which Favre, somehow, did.

It is a story of a young, hotshot quarterback who fell out of favor in Atlanta, the team that drafted him in 1991, and landed in Green Bay with a new coach and a franchise desperately trying to regain the magic of 30 years earlier. And it's the story that says, sometimes, dreams really do come true.

Brett Favre was always one of the kids who was bigger than life. Even as a little kid he was the quarterback who led his pee wee team to the prestigious "Mullet Bowl." At North Central High, where he played for his dad Irvin, he was an option quarterback who yearned to throw the ball but played within a system.

At Southern Mississippi, he was known as much for his remarkable recuperative powers as his ability to play football. Indeed, his national profile increased dramatically in July, 1990, when he was in serious car accident and had to have 30 inches of his intestines removed. Not even a month later, he was on the field and leading the Golden Eagles to an upset win over Alabama.

So anyone who didn't know how tough Favre was before learned quickly after that. In four seasons at Southern Miss, Favre (whose name was frequently and horrendously mispronounced, mostly by Easterners) led the Golden Eagles to 29 wins, two bowl victories and an MVP award in the East-West Shrine Game.

He also caught the eye of a New York Jets scout by the name of Ron Wolf, who badly wanted his team to draft the young quarterback. But the Jets never got the chance as he was taken in the second round by the Falcons, the 33rd pick overall and third quarterback selected behind Dan McGwire and Todd Marinovich.

Favre languished with the Falcons as a rookie, frequently raising the ire of coach Jerry Glanville for his carefree ways. Often, Favre would stun observers that year by taking footballs and firing them into the upper decks of stadiums. It was the only action Favre really saw.

When Wolf took over in 1992 as the Packers' general manager, one of his first moves was to trade for Favre, and on February 10, he gave up a first-round pick to get him. The rest, as they say, is history.

THE SETTING

The legend began on September 20, 1992, when Favre subbed for the injured Don Majkowski and led the Packers to a last-minute win over Cincinnati. There would be many, many other games like that—too many, in fact, to recount.

But Favre proved early on that injuries wouldn't stop him from playing the game he loved. In one of the greatest performances, he shook off a severely sprained left ankle in 1995 to play against the Bears.

"I didn't practice at all the whole week," Favre said. "Usually I do something just to get a feel for it, but that week I didn't do anything. The ankle wasn't broken, but it was purple and yellow. I've actually had surgery on that ankle since, and while I'm not saying what happened on that particular day caused the surgery, it didn't help. But my ankle has never been the same."

In a key game at home against Chicago, Favre, with an ankle taped so heavily it resembled a cast, threw five touchdown passes in a 35-28 win.

"I'm not the most mobile guy to begin with, but I really couldn't move in that game," he said. "I really had to rely on stuff I've got in my arsenal but never want to use. In fact it made me be a pocket passer, and I'm never quite sure if I can do that."

That sprained ankle had come the week before in another demoralizing loss to the Minnesota Vikings in the Metrodome.

Brett Favre. *Jonathan Daniel/Getty Images*

Even then, that dome had developed into a house of horrors for the Packers.

In 1992, with a playoff berth on the line, the Packers were clobbered 27-7. In 1993, a last-second desperation completion to a guy named Eric Guliford had led to a last-second loss. In 1994, the Packers lost in overtime.

And in 1995, it was even worse. With Favre and backup Ty Detmer both out with injuries, the quarterbacking duties fell to journeyman T.J. Rubley. Still, somehow, the Packers were in control and had the ball and the lead late in the game. But inexplicably, Rubley called an audible on a Holmgren run play and tried a pass that was intercepted. The Vikings came back to tie the game and then win it with a field goal in overtime.

Rubley was gone the next day.

"It just seemed like we were cursed," Favre said.

THE GAME OF MY LIFE
By Brett Favre

I don't know. For other guys it might be easy to pick one game. The obvious choice would be the Super Bowl, but even games we didn't win or games where I didn't play as well as others, every one of them has been memorable. That's probably why I've been as successful as I have been for so long—I've enjoyed the hell out of every one.

But last year in Minnesota may rank, in my opinion, as one of the all-time best. When I've felt my best I've had terrible games over there, so of all the games I played in Minnesota, the one this past year would have been easiest one for everyone to say, "Well, they ain't got a chance. Favre can't play when he's healthy, and now he's going to try to play with a broken thumb?"

We had just gotten beaten in St. Louis in a dome and I'd heard all the talk about domes, but I never paid much attention to it. But the stats don't lie. So I was determined I was going to play. I was telling myself most the time, "You're stupid. Of all the times you could actually back out of a game and no one would question it, this is it. You've got a broken thumb. You obviously can sit this one out and not catch any grief over it." But I really wanted to play and redeem myself, broken thumb or not.

When I knew I was going to play, I thought, "How am I going to play with a splint? Hell, you can't play with a splint on your throwing hand. And of all places in Minnesota."

And Mike Sherman, he's telling me all week and putting pressure on me saying, "If you can play, great, because you've always played great coming off injury." And I said, "Mike, now you're putting pressure on me of all places." He was real optimistic. I wasn't as optimistic, but I was confident. I said that if I'm going to play, I'm going to play. But to play the way I did, and obviously win the game, which we haven't done there a lot, ranks as one of the best.

I went out early that morning and went out for a walk-through and we were just trying some different stuff, because the previous week we were off. The splint was not my idea, but they wanted to tape it up, and I said that I needed the least amount of tape, because I need to be able to try to feel the ball as much as I possibly could. I knew the splint would keep the thumb from moving. So I said let's Super Glue the splint to the back of my thumb. That way if the tape comes off, it should keep me from using a lot of tape. And it did do that. It took us three days to get that splint off, and we never did it again. We used nail polish remover, you name it. It got to the point where it almost pulled my thumbnail off.

But that morning, messing around with different tape jobs, I was able to throw the ball fine. But throwing with a broken thumb and no one chasing you and you're able to just kind of concentrate is one thing. It's different than when they're chasing you and all eyes are upon you. It's a different ballgame, even with a good thumb. I was confident I could throw the ball. But it's just a different ballgame when they're shooting live bullets at you.

But as the game progressed, I was making plays I hadn't attempted in practice. I was probably as surprised as anyone afterwards with the throws I made. I was able to kind of go through the

game without really thinking about it. Six or seven games into
wearing the splint I thought back to that Minnesota game, and I
thought, "I have no idea how I did it," because my thumb bothered me the whole year. It got a little bit better and a little bit better, and a little bit better, but I don't know I did it because it had-
n't even been two weeks since I'd broken it. And six or seven weeks
after I'd broken it, the X-rays looked the same as the day after I'd
broken it. So, for a lot of reasons, that win was important, because
the odds were definitely against me that game.

I put a lot of thought into that week, really the two weeks. So
much went through my mind those two weeks. When the game
was over against St. Louis, I was upset that we'd lost and I had no

**In a career with innumerable highlights, leading the
Packers to a win over the Vikings at the Metrodome despite
a broken thumb in 2003 rates the highest.** *AP/WWP*

idea my thumb was broken until the next day. But I played, for the most part, fairly well. My thumb was killing me, but I figured it was just bruised.

But going back on the plane I was thinking that it was not looking good this year and that's not even knowing my thumb was broken. When I found out it was broken, I thought, "This ain't good; it's going be one of those years." I really thought I was done. That's the first broken bone I'd ever had, and in my throwing hand at that.

But I told Mike and [team doctor] Pat [McKenzie] and [head trainer] Pepper [Burruss] that I thought I could play. They said, "You have a broken thumb." And I said, "Well, I had a broken thumb the whole day yesterday." Had I known it, I probably wouldn't have played. But now that I knew I could play and actually played fairly well against St. Louis, I thought I could play [against the Vikings]. Had I known in St. Louis, I would have played differently, protected it and stuff.

But more than anything, I just wanted to go over there and win. Hell, I hadn't had much success in there, and I considered it a huge challenge, good thumb or not, to go over there and win. I didn't look at it like, "Well, if we lose, everybody will say he had a broken thumb and this time he has an excuse." I didn't look at it that way. The easy games, everyone wants to play in those, and I knew the odds were against me. But I just considered it a huge challenge.

GAME RESULT

To understand the importance of the Vikings game, it's important to go back two weeks to Edward Jones in St. Louis where the Packers lost 34-24 and where Favre broke his thumb after hitting the helmet of guard Mike Wahle.

Favre broke the thumb in the second quarter, yet continued to play. And though the Packers lost, Favre played well, completing 23 of 32 passes for 268 yards with two touchdowns and one interception.

With the bye week looming, Favre figured he could play against the Vikings, who had led the NFC North comfortably but were now starting to lose steam. Favre knew if he could play, it would provide an emotional lift the team desperately needed.

And it wasn't as though he put up terrific numbers against the Vikings. He completed 18 of 28 passes for 194 yards and threw two touchdown passes to Javon Walker and one to Ahman Green. But it was more how he managed the game, took the plays that were available to him and never put himself, or the team, in trouble. Then he relied on the running game that piled up 261 yards, including 137 by Green.

It wasn't an easy win, because it never is in the Metrodome, where half the crowd is for the Packers and the other half is ramped up to a fever pitch to see the Packers lose.

But Favre's touchdown pass to Walker and a Ryan Longwell field goal with 2:37 to play gave the Packers a seemingly comfortable 30-20 lead. The Vikings scored again to make it close, but the Packers got away with a 30-27 victory.

The importance was obvious. It showed the Packers could win in a dome against their longtime nemesis. It showed Favre could play with a bad thumb. And it showed that the division race, which had seemed over, was far from it. The win brought the Packers within two games of the Vikings, and they had the easier schedule down the stretch.

And in the end, it made all the difference as the Packers slipped in to win the title on the last day of the season.

WHAT BECAME OF BRETT FAVRE?

Favre signed a new contract in 2001 that will, for all practical purposes, keep him a Packer forever. And that's as it should be.

He has said he will play for as long as the game remains fun and as long as the Packers have a chance to win. He hinted at retirement during the 2002 season but backed off those statements in 2003 and had one of his best seasons ever.

The Packers still have no idea who will replace Favre, but it's an issue they can live with as long as Favre continues to play at a high level. It's believed he will play at least two more years, though he won't say for sure. And with Favre, he could retire next week or play five more years.

He continues to play a vital role in the Green Bay community. His Brett Favre Forward Foundation has raised millions of dollars for disadvantaged kids, and his annual softball game in Appleton drew a record 8,000 people in 2004.

In his spare time, he plays golf and takes care of the 460 acres on which he built a new home in Hattiesburg. He said repeatedly he won't play football for any other team but the Packers.

Whenever he does retire, he will have to wait five years, but he will have a spot reserved in the Pro Football Hall of Fame.

Celebrate the Heroes of Wisconsin Sports
and Professional Football in These Other Releases from Sports Publishing

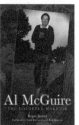

Al McGuire:
The Colorful Warrior
by Roger Jaynes

- 6 x 9 hardcover
- 275 pages
- eight-page photo section
- $24.95

Riddell Presents:
The Gridiron's Greatest
Quarterbacks
by Jonathan Rand

- 9 x 12 hardcover
- 140 pages
- color photos throughout
- $24.95

Tales from the Packers
Sideline
by Chuck Carlson

- 5.5 x 8.25 hardcover
- 200 pages
- photos throughout
- $19.95
- (2003 release)

Like a Rose: A Thoughtful
Celebration of Football
by Rick Telander

- 5.5 x 7 hardcover • 160 pages
- 8-page color-photo section
- $19.95 • Includes bonus
"Beyond the Book" DVD!

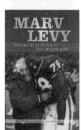

Marv Levy: Where Else
Would You Rather Be?
by Marv Levy

- 6 x 9 hardcover
- 250 pages
- photos throughout
- $24.95

Legends of the Dallas
Cowboys
by Cody Monk

- 8.5 x 11 hardcover
- 180 pages
- color photos throughout
- $24.95

The Golden Voices
of Football
by Ted Patterson

- 10.25 x 10.25 hardcover
- photos/illustrations
  throughout
- 200 pages • $29.95
- Includes an audio CD!

Steve McMichael's Tales
from the Bears Sideline
by Steve McMichael
with Phil Arvia

- 5.5 x 8.25 hardcover
- 200 pages
- photos throughout
- $19.95

Matt Kenseth:
Above and Beyond
by Matt Kenseth
with Kelley Maruszewski

- 10 x 10 hardcover
- 160 pages
- color photos throughout
- $24.95

Dante Hall: X-Factor
by Dante Hall with Bill
Althaus

- 8.5 x 11 hardcover
- 128 pages
- color photos throughout
- $24.95

To order at any time, please call toll-free **877-424-BOOK (2665)**.
For fast service and quick delivery, order on-line at **www.SportsPublishingLLC.com**.